Sol Plaatje European Union
Poetry Anthology

Vol VI

# The Sol Plaatje European Union Poetry Anthology

## Volume VI

Selected by Goodenough Mashego,
Thabiso Mohare, Pieter Odendaal,
Mongane Wally Serote

*The views and opinions expressed in this publication are not necessarily those of the funder.*

The Jacana Literary Foundation is greatful to the *Mail & Guardian* for the support they have provided.

First published by Jacana Media (Pty) Ltd in 2016

10 Orange Street
Sunnyside
Auckland Park 2092
South Africa
+2711 628 3200
www.jacana.co.za

© Individual authors, 2016
© Cover image: Lindeka Qampi from *Inside My Heart* series, 2015.
Courtesy Erdmann Contemporary

All rights reserved.

ISBN 978-1-4314-2483-2

Cover design by Shawn Paikin
Set in Ehrhardt 11/13pt
Printed and bound by Bidvest Data
Job no. 002850

See a complete list of Jacana titles at www.jacana.co.za

# Contents

Foreword *Dr Mongane Wally Serote* . . . . . . . . . . . . . . . . . . . . . . . xi
A message from the sponsors
   *The European Union* . . . . . . . . . . . . . . . . . . . . . . . . . . . . . . . . xv
   *The Mail & Guardian* . . . . . . . . . . . . . . . . . . . . . . . . . . . . . . . xvi
A note on translation by Goodenough Mashego . . . . . . . . . . . xvii
A tribute to our country's original spoken word poets . . . . . . . . . xx
LIKE A LOG, *Jim Pascual Agustin* . . . . . . . . . . . . . . . . . . . . . . . . 1
ANGEL, *Caroline F Archer* . . . . . . . . . . . . . . . . . . . . . . . . . . . . . . 2
HOTNOTS-KÁNON, *Caroline F Archer* . . . . . . . . . . . . . . . . . . . 4
   MANTIS CANON, *an English translation by Pieter Odendaal* . . . 6
BATTLEGROUND, *Mutinta Bbenkele* . . . . . . . . . . . . . . . . . . . . . 8
EDEN'S KNELL, *Tanisha Bhana* . . . . . . . . . . . . . . . . . . . . . . . 10
IN THE MOOD TO MONKEY, *Zéwande Bk Bhengu* . . . . . . . . 11
KLEEDREPETISIE, *Rene Bohnen* . . . . . . . . . . . . . . . . . . . . . . . 13
   DRESS REHEARSAL, *an English translation by*
   *Pieter Odendaal* . . . . . . . . . . . . . . . . . . . . . . . . . . . . . . . . . . . . 14
PIPE DREAM, *Kathryn Clare Botes* . . . . . . . . . . . . . . . . . . . . . 15
THE THIRST, *Dianne Case* . . . . . . . . . . . . . . . . . . . . . . . . . . . . 16
REFUGEE, *Christine Coates* . . . . . . . . . . . . . . . . . . . . . . . . . . . . 18
TERRA NULLIUS – THE MARIKANA SYMPHONY,
   *Christine Coates* . . . . . . . . . . . . . . . . . . . . . . . . . . . . . . . . . . . . 19
"WINTER COLD", *Bella (B-lyrical) Cox* . . . . . . . . . . . . . . . . . 21
CHOKING, *Bella (B-lyrical) Cox* . . . . . . . . . . . . . . . . . . . . . . . . 23
ALL CHANGE, *Lise Day* . . . . . . . . . . . . . . . . . . . . . . . . . . . . . . 26
THE ARCHBISHOP'S LAMENT, *Graham Dukas* . . . . . . . . . . 27
METAMORPHOSIS, *Graham Dukas* . . . . . . . . . . . . . . . . . . . . . 28
PLACE OF THE JACKAL, *Elaine Edwards* . . . . . . . . . . . . . . . . 29

IN RESPONSE TO SEEING AN AFRICAN
    WOMAN ABBA A DOG ON FACEBOOK, *Connie Fick* .... 31
RE KWALA TSE DI SWA, *Tshepo Gaerupe* ................ 32
    WE WRITE NEW ONES, *an English translation*
    *by Goodenough Mashego* ................................ 35
HLAL' APH' EMZINI NGOB' IINKOMO ZIYATHETHA,
    *Nobuntu Gantana* ...................................... 38
        STAY IN YOUR MARITAL HOME, FOR CATTLE
        SPEAKS VOLUMES, *an English translation*
        *by Vuyokazi Ngemntu*.............................. 40
DRAGONS AND FLAMES, *Sarah Godsell* ................ 42
MOTHER AND DAUGHTER WALK, *Dorian Haarhoff* ..... 44
FATHER AND SON SONG, *Dorian Haarhoff*............. 45
FLESH AND BONE TANGO, *Dorian Haarhoff* ............ 47
COMING HOME, *Kerry Hammerton* ..................... 48
X-MAS TIDE, *Jay Heale*................................ 50
ABA TE (CARRY ME), *Tracey (Khadija) Heeger*............ 51
SLOW COOKER, *Heidi Elisabeth Henning* ................. 54
PEOPLE OF THE SKY, *Thapelo Hlongwane* ............... 55
MAMBHELE'S HARVEST, *Siphokazi Jonas*............... 58
WEEKLY SERVICE, *Siphokazi Jonas*..................... 62
I AM BEAUTIFUL, *Fiona Khan* ....................... 65
CLASS, *Musawenkosi Khanyile* .......................... 67
CHURCH, *Musawenkosi Khanyile* ....................... 68
OMRING, *Lara Kirsten* ................................ 70
    ENCIRCLING, *an English translation by Pieter Odendaal*...... 72
RIBBONS ON THE FENCE, *Lynne Kloot*................. 74
NTSO YAMATHILE, *Nomnikelo Komanisi* ................ 75
    KIDNEY OF THE SO-AND-SO CLAN, *an English*
    *translation by Vuyokazi Ngemntu* ......................... 77

THERE'S A ME THAT'S STILL
NOT FREE, *Portia Mabaso* .......................... 78
MOTHERS WARN YOUR DAUGHTERS, *Portia Mabaso* ... 80
HIP HOP, *Songeziwe Mahlangu* ......................... 82
APARTHEID IN THE SKY, *Patrick Maitland* .............. 83
THEY CAME, *Patrick Maitland* ........................ 84
SALUTE TO KLIPSPRUIT RIVER, *Maishe Maponya*....... 86
THE TRC – ON THE BOX, *Maishe Maponya* .............. 90
THE POWER-POINT POET, *Maishe Maponya* ............ 94
CAPE TOWN, *Charles Marriott*......................... 96
JOHANNES SI BHEKE, *Kela Maswabi*.................. 99
   JOHANNES LOOK AT US, *an English translation by*
   *Goodenough Mashego*................................ 101
UPHAHLA, *Zongezile Theophilus Matshoba* ............... 103
   THE ROOF, *an English translation by Vuykazi Ngemntu* .... 104
GO DIKGAITŠEDI TŠA LEFSIFSI, *Katise Mawela*....... 105
   TO THE LADIES OF THE NIGHT, *an English translation*
   *by Goodenough Mashego* ............................... 106
IKASI LAMI, *Ongezwa Mbele*......................... 107
PUINHOOP, *Marthé Mcloud*.......................... 108
   RUINS, *an English translation by Pieter Odendaal* .......... 109
HO THABA BA ILENG, *Thabiso Mofokeng*............... 110
   HAPPY ARE THOSE GONE, *an English translation*
   *by Goodenough Mashego* ............................... 114
DIFAQANE, *Maneo Refiloe Mohale*..................... 118
GAUTA O JA BATHO, *Tsietsi Mokhele*.................. 120
   GOLD CONSUMES HUMANS, *an English translation by*
   *Goodenough Mashego*................................ 122
YET MORE STONES, *George Momogos* ................. 124
VERGANGENHEITSBEWAELTIGUNG, *Jackie Mondi*.... 125
A HUNGRY STOMACH HAS NO EARS, *Jackie Mondi*.... 126

| | |
|---|---|
| VARIATIONS IN COLOUR, *Nedine Moonsamy* | 127 |
| LANIWANI, *Moses Mtileni* | 129 |
| THE HOUSE WE BUILT, *Sifiso Mtshali* | 130 |
| "TO MOS DEF IN THE WOOLWORTHS QUEUE", *Nick Mulgrew* | 133 |
| FOUR MINUTES, *Luthando Ncayiyana* | 136 |
| THE BARKSOLE MAN, *Pamela Newham* | 137 |
| TO THOSE FLUTTERING BEINGS, *Mandla Robert Ngakane* | 138 |
| NOT ANOTHER NURSE'S TALE, *Mandla Robert Ngakane* | 139 |
| A THANKLESS LABOUR, *Vuyokazi Ngemntu* | 141 |
| THEY NEVER DIED, *Bomikazi Njoloza* | 143 |
| ILIZWE LAM, *Amanda Nodada* | 144 |
| MY COUNTRY, *an English translation by Vuyokazi Ngemntu* | 147 |
| CASSETTE, *Sihle Ntuli* | 150 |
| "REFLECTION", *Lazola Pambo* | 151 |
| BLACK JOY, *Koleka Putuma* | 153 |
| RESURRECTION, *Koleka Putuma* | 154 |
| BEDTIME STORIES FOR OUR LITTLE GIRLS, *Sibongile Ralana* | 155 |
| A PENNY FOR YOUR THOUGHTS, *Sibongile Ralana* | 156 |
| POWER, *Arja Salafranca* | 157 |
| COLLATERAL DAMAGE, *Ferdie Schaller* | 158 |
| THE BURNING MAN, *Ferdie Schaller* | 159 |
| BOOTS FOR LITTLE BOYS, *Ferdie Schaller* | 161 |
| OOGAF, *Karin Schimke* | 163 |
| AT A GLANCE, *an English translation by Pieter Odendaal* | 164 |
| UNCLE TOM, *Kori Sefeane* | 165 |
| AUSCHWITS, *Kori Sefeane* | 169 |

| | |
|---|---|
| FIX ME, *Sinazo Somhlahlo* | 172 |
| a revolution, *Caitlin Spring* | 175 |
| MINE WILL BE OF AFRICA, *David C Steyn* | 176 |
| EVEN BIRDS, *Caitlin Stobie* | 178 |
| REFUGEE, *Louella Sullivan* | 180 |
| THEATRE OF HEARTS, *Elizabeth Trew* | 181 |
| STHANDWA SAM', *Lesego Tsoho* | 182 |
|    MY LOVE, *an English translation by Goodenough Mashego* | 185 |
| NGIYABONGA MAMA, *Lesego Tsoho* | 188 |
|    THANK YOU MAMA, *an English translation by Goodenough Mashego* | 191 |
| IN MY CUPBOARD, *Troydon Wainwright* | 194 |
| A WEDDING POEM, *Troydon Wainwright* | 195 |
| INVESTMENT RETURNS, *Athol Williams* | 196 |
| VISIT AT TEA TIME, *Athol Williams* | 197 |
| missing, *Sue Woodward* | 200 |
| | |
| Afterword *Sabata-mpho Mokae* | 201 |
| Biographies | 205 |
| What is the European Union (EU)? | 226 |

# Foreword

When you read this Volume VI, if you have heard about our country, South Africa, you will be trapped like a bee, worse still, like a fly trapped in a pool of syrup. You will try to understand what change is – what does it mean? You may walk away confused; or bewildered, unable even to wonder, or waft or wander because your mind will be boggled. Your mind has to be boggled. Change does carry within it both the past and the present. It has to, because it is razor sharp. It cuts across everything; it reveals the insides of this thing called truth, which is at all times relative.

These South African poets have understood something. They live inside or between the past and the present as they seek the future. In their honest and sincere efforts to find a way to that future, they find that the future remains a dream, which is a hope but, because it is almost unreal, cannot be lived. When a new generation begins to emerge, the old and the new begin to speak in tongues to each other. They do not understand each other. The one generation is a slice of the past and the present, and may be sceptical about the future; yet the new is a slice of the present bored by the past, being impatient with the future, which takes time to reveal itself. If the past is not listened to carefully, it seems to pale into being irrelevant but remains present and staring. The present is forever present in the past and into the future, it forever shimmers in both.

If you read the poems in this volume, be careful. They hold the present by the scruff and threaten it. They seem poisonous; they seem deadly. These poems threaten hope. These poems, in all of their body, all of them, as poems together, are real and relative, are elegant and most sophisticated, better than philosophy. They do not waffle; no, the word is also, they do not mean words. But like philosophy, they search deep. This volume of poems cuts reality into relativity. You cannot say you know anything if you do not know yourself, the poets say; they say, you cannot say you know you if you do not know your past; also, you cannot know yourself if you do know what is outside of you, what is external to you, which is also informed and reflects the past, the present and the future. This is a necessary tension. This tension will grow. It will transform itself, to transform everything else around itself and itself into a rupture; to become change. Our understanding this is our understanding of how change evolves, to become revolt. If this nation has not revolted, it is evolving to revolt, the poets say.

Racism is violent. Sexism is violent. Democracy is real, but intangible, also because racism and sexism are present and do exist. Racism, like sexism, are social expressions of exploitation, which depend on being, by dehumanising – what the Christians call demonising, which also means corrupting, like tribalism does. Caesar demands and claims everything which he claims is his alone! Therefore the so-called democracy, which will forever attempt to keep together what must rupture not to rupture, though antagonistic, though present and unreal, finds that everywhere, society, social actions are clinging to what they know; social actions in their complexity and eternal motion become afraid, are afraid lest change means ripping and rupture of social privilege acquired through power: subtle, cunning or brutal.

The poets have this instinct they have; through it, they have gathered things which tell them that mmmmm something is a-changing, they have picked it up and they feel it and they are expressing so many things which in essence are lived by people and the society. The society keeps holding on to what it knows – the past – the poets say. Because poets also have the instinct not to say things too soon because they learn things slowly, but also because they have observed society's mal-reactions, and because they know too well too that Caesar kills, the poets in this volume sing songs. The present cannot hold. The poets keep saying. Asked, they cunningly say – so says the present when it understands the past and the future. It is true that poets know something about timelines – they do. What shall motivate whomever to resolve the dialectic? It will be resolved by whom, how? When will it be resolved? Don't you know that procrastination is the place where fools and cowards live? The poets ask, in subtle ways, but they have too spoken boldly, it is just that they are never ever heard, or, they are heard late because they are never read. They do not, as all of us can see and hear, tire though! Read this volume.

Sometimes, at times the poets say, there seems to be a time-bomb here. This ignorance of the captains, which plays at being itself, when in reality it is either fear, hopeless hope, amnesia, helplessness or cunning and clinging to power, it is the reality of power which corrupts – history, the poets know, says so.

This unknowing to answer critical questions, or the pretence to do so, means that the present and the future cannot hold. If lessons are not learnt; have not been learnt and if the origins of change elude the captains, and if the extent of change and its complex context is not known and understood, as procrastination defines itself as being what it is – it will also sound like a time-bomb. The poets know this, they have always known it, by how they see, hear and feel it – then, like healers, the poets sing, beat the drums and dance to the rhythm of their tongues – after all, they are South Africans.

*Mongane Wally Serote*
*August 2016*

# A message from the sponsors

## The European Union

Once again, South African poets have heeded the call and have, in their numbers, participated in this year's Sol Plaatje European Union Poetry Award. The past five resulting anthologies have provided a wonderful view on South Africa: its past, its present, its future. There have been uplifting poems, some dark and reflective works, some beautifully descriptive of South African society.

Despite most entries being submitted in English, what makes this competition unlike any other is that it invites entries in any of South Africa's eleven official languages. The European Union, too, is a multi-cultural society with some 24 official languages. It is thus a privilege for the EU Delegation to South Africa to be associated with this initiative, now in its sixth edition.

I am delighted that this year the Mail & Guardian has come on board as the media partner and I take this opportunity to express my sincere thanks to the Jacana Literary Foundation for its continued commitment to this project.

*Marcus Cornaro*
*Ambassador of the European Union to South Africa*

## The Mail & Guardian

South African public life can be relentless. At the *Mail & Guardian*, we are too aware of that. We are constantly bombarded with game-changing moments and seismic events. When your country's news ricochets around the world on a regular basis, it's easy to become numb.

Against this backdrop poetry isn't just important: it is necessary.

It is our writers who tell us our stories and shape our narratives. And it is our poets who breathe magic and meaning into our lives.

From large public machinations to small private moments, South Africa's poetry has sung the deepest song in our hearts when mere sentences would no longer do.

Poetry has guided us through that first great transition to democracy, led by a generation of poets we still stand in awe of.

And now more than ever a younger generation is raising urgent voices, questioning everything and pushing us into the future, whether we like it or not. In this climate it is the next generation of poets that we must listen to.

The Sol Plaatje European Union Poetry Award has, since 2011, provided a space for exactly that. The *Mail & Guardian* is proud to partner with this anthology and the awards, as we recognise not just the voices of the future, but the country we will become.

*Verashni Pillay*
*Editor-in-chief*

# A note on translation by Goodenough Mashego

Every language is rich when its pulp is sucked from the source. And every language has got its own way of standing proud like a peacock; especially when utilised by proud practitioners of it. Those, like me, whose introduction to authentic Afrikaans *gedigtes* was through Breyten Breytenbach's 'Bufallo Bill'; or those who loved Eugene Terre'blanche's musing poetry or even Matthews Phosa's surface 'Deur Die Oog van n Naald' will attest to the colour that comes with every word written, even when the poet does not use rhymes or metaphors. It's easy to fall in love with Afrikaans *gedigtes* when the language used is less-bastardised and sticks closely to ancestral Dutch.

The same can be said about English poetry by twentieth-century Jewish poets. Their flirting with archaic Yiddish words and phrases gives such renditions an original Middle Eastern feel. Which helps us understand that William Shakespeare was not a genius; he was just comfortable with language. He became a famous bard due to the linguistic laissez-faire of his time. That freedom inspired the poetry of his generation and those after that.

African indigenous languages are like a painter's brush whose stroke across canvas leaves an indelible mark that can only enhance their poetic aesthetic. There's no indigenous language that is void of idioms, proverbs, euphemisms, metaphors, etc., that in many communities have become part of everyday talk. That daily nectar should not be sacrificed in the writing of poetry since this artform is the pinnacle of linguistic glory. Hence the issue of a 'poetic license'. Poets writing with prizes and literary awards in mind should not make the mistake of diluting the beauty and richness of their languages for appraisal expediency. Literary judges will always adjudicate poetic output on the strength of its original language. The late Mazisi Kunene and Mafika Gwala raised the bar through which isiZulu poetry will always be interrogated.

In cases of literary adjudications, loose English translations, which often accompany indigenous poetry, lack the capacity to reflect the same colour. They are weak replicas. Weakened reflections of God's glory. That, however, does not mean they are unnecessary. The challenge with translation has always been whether it stays true to the text or the language and its traditions. If a Zulu poet writes '*indoda yindoda ngenkomu zayo*', does that mean saying 'we judge a man by his wealth' is wrong? No, for communication expediency it is accurate since it acknowledges that herds of cattle translate into wealth in African communities.

Even on issues of *lobola/magadi* we still say 'a man must have cattle to marry' even though the transaction is in money.

So, a lot of pulp gets lost in translating indigenous language poetry because there's no way such a translation will ever be as poetic as the original text. As it happened with the Holy Bible the indigenous versions of which are oceans apart from the original Greek and Hebrew text, it is happening with contemporary poetry. My advice, indigenous language poets should not even try to translate their work or weaken it for easy access; the denser the better.

This, however, should not make indigenous poets despair. It is reason enough to infuse their poetry with more traditional nuances, mystic and depth, because not only is the exercise about preserving a language in its wealth, it is also receiving the baton from ancestors. Shakespeare makes sense in English; just try translating it into an indigenous language and you will get my point.

# A tribute to our country's original spoken word poets

This anthology delves into the languages, experiences and sentiments that unite and divide us as South Africans. Much of the poetry featured is topical, but there are things we share even with the oldest poets who walked here. The same heavens arch over us as we go about our daily lives below. Here, through this English translation of a San poem, we pay tribute to the legacy of the original spoken word poets, the "clans of people – men, women, and children – long since become stars".

### Sun, moon and stars

The sun that is down
comes out of the mountains
It will stand there, above us,
high in the heavens. Come morning,
the sun will once more go walking
across the great skies.

The moon, hunter's moon,
will come out of that mountain;
it too will go walking, waxing
and waning across the great skies.

The star we await,
that star will come after, out of the mountain,

it will climb, quick like the others,
rising, striding, across the great skies.

Many stars are in heaven.
There are whole clans of people –
men, women, and children –
long since become stars.

And now the star woman,
see, she starts rising,
comes again like a mother
leading out her star child,
while the man star follows,
his child star running after.
If the sun is long down,
if the young moon has set,
the star mother will come,
come out of the mountain,
will lead her star child –
even, as you see,
he runs away for a while,
runs now, for a little, into a cloud.[1]

---

[1] Watson, S. *Return of the Moon: Versions from the /Xam.* (Cape Town: The Carrefour Press, 1991)

The origin of these poems is an extensive ethnographic record known as the Bleek and Lloyd collection, a testimony of folklore, songs and stories that formed part of the /Xam oral tradition (the /Xam being one linguistic group of the Bushman who lived in southern Africa in the nineteenth century). The testimony was narrated by three men, //Kabbo, /Han≠kasso and Dia!kwain, and transcribed by Dr W H Bleek and Lucy Lloyd in the 1870s. Watson 're-cast' excerpts from this testimony into poetry, a complex process he recounts in his original publication, *Return of the Moon: Versions from the /Xam.*

# LIKE A LOG

"I'm not going to tell you another story,
my boy. You laugh too loud," grandfather said
as I begged. His voice sounded
like it was coming from the village well

before it was blasted. The stories
he told came from a time when the sky
was not yet something to be feared.
His eyes, clouded with cataract,
only saw white shadows.

But he could sense when someone
was stirring awake. He began to fade
into the damp wood. I whispered to him,
"I am afraid of the dark and the sound
of water splashing against the sides

of the boat." Grandfather held
my small hands and then patted
the tied up bundle mother left me
before they threw her overboard.

      JIM PASCUAL AGUSTIN

# ANGEL

They have invented this game of make-believe;
Teacher and her, to provide relief;
some variety of Houdini escapism.
It is a mind-game providing endless possibility
and the two of them are good at utilising this.
They pretend to assume control over their destiny.
Teacher loves Angel for her resourcefulness.
She adores her for her openness.

Angel is seven and skin and bone and a bit undefined like
   pollen.
She develops severe cramps when faced with numbers;
the two of them have always favoured literacy.

School mornings Angel skips towards her,
fancy-free and loose of limb.
Teacher feels bird-song in her hug.
Life sparks from Angel like an electric field
and disperses grown-up mists of anxiety.
Angel's arms open like landing gear:

*Angel, let's fly away,*
*Where are you taking me today?*

*To my auntie Biba in Vosloo Rust, just behind the spaza.*
*We shall visit the sangoma*
*and take turns carrying little Simphiwe.*

Angel has a small body: thin like the thread
her auntie cuts from the Spaza bags.

She makes strange fowls
with fan-shaped feathers.
Teacher notices the bruise Angel brought to school this
 morning;
fingerprints along the skinny arm and the last bruise
clutched away under the bottle of Oros in the girl's
 armpit.
Today, her eyes remain distraught like those of a kitten
that has seen unthinkable things,
Angel has little to say.

Death plays an inventive game in squatter camps and lean-
 to's.
This game is called noughts and crosses.
More often than not, it scores three crosses in quick
 succession.

Her shadow does not cross the slab of sunshine that slants
 my schoolroom door.
She has outgrown me.

CAROLINE F ARCHER

# HOTNOTS-KÁNON

Vaak het vatmerke oor die ligkring begin maak
toe 'n fyn segment,
uitgebrande filament
tafelgebed kom doen bo die bed.

Skielik, skommelend in skuim,
het sy haar vlerke oopgeskrik,
uitdagend verseg om te vlieg
en op dik dye gewieg.

Teen die grys van die kamermuur
word sy 'n godinnetjie
en sy argitektuur in haar driehoek-koppie
'n hele mierkolonie.

Wirrend, onhoorbaar-sag smakkend.
in sagte skuim wiegend,
sit sy 'n paringsmaat in duisend bedebriefies
te verslind.

"Jy *ag jou vernamer as die maanhaar wat by droë lope buk*
(*die Nossob en die Auob*),
*hoër as die flaminke,*" (so praat die San)
"*wat dikwels in verwaaide panne staan.*

*Saans hou jy die maan dop,*
*verhef jou bo die rokerige vure,*
*klim moeisaam die kremetart op,*
*om die son uit sy takke te lig.*"

*"Maar,"* so klik die Nharo in die Okavango,
*"wanneer ons rotsteken teen die klip,*
*dan verweer jy, stokkerig, alleen-ek*
*as* 'n *klein houtbas-insek."*

Hou uit jou stekelrige voorklou
om die pofklein maan,
die doringdons,
in vas te hou.

                CAROLINE F ARCHER

# MANTIS CANON

Somnolence had left touch-marks around the halo
when a fine segment,
burnt-out filament
came to say grace above the bed.

Suddenly, wiggling in foam,
she frightened her wings open,
defiantly refused to fly
and jiggled on thick thighs.

Against the grey of the bedroom wall
she becomes a small goddess
and she architectures in her triangle-head
a whole colony of ants

Whirring, smacking inaudibly soft.
cradling in light foam,
she sits, devouring a coital partner into
a thousand prayer-poems.

"You deem yourself worthier than the maned lion who
    crouches at dry streams
(the Nossob and the Auob),
higher than the flamingo," (so the San say)
"who often stands in windswept pans.

At night you observe the moon,
exalt yourself above the smoky fires,
laboriously climb up the baobab,
to lift the sun out of its branches."

"But," click the Nharo in the Okavango,
"when we rock-draw on stone,
you erode, stalkily, lonesome-I,
into a small bark beetle ."

Extend your prickly front talon
in order for the puff-small moon,
the thorny-fluff, to be held.

*Translated from the Afrikaans original – Caroline F Archer's*
*'Hotnots-kánon' – by Pieter Odendaal*

# BATTLEGROUND

The battleground that is mother and daughter
You are not the first to choke on the poison ivy that is her bitterness
You are not the cause for the lies that are meant to protect you from who she really is
You are a lifetime of hard decisions and sacrifice
If you do not make them worth doing, if your actions do not speak to that pain
You'll be worth fighting with, in attempts to fight for
You are one of her many scars
The shattering truth when you realise that you were birthed from a broken star
When for the entirety of your existence
You believe that she was a full moon
Bright and gawked at when in view.
This truth will rip at the graceful wind that once glided into your lungs
Turn it into an icy legion of daggers relentlessly piercing at your chest
Your touch will replicate the sickly version of all the tattered love you ever received and she ...
She will hurl the hurt she buried deep in her heart
"I can't believe I bore you" she said
Looking straight into my eyes
"I can't believe I bore you"
Words from decades ago that still stop the earth's rotation when I recall them
Call it being human
Call it a reaction to my attitude

But nothing, nothing should ever hear of the regret of its creation
I have chosen to crouch deep into this trench of hurt
And here I will remain whilst you relentlessly aim and shoot
Hoping that I will move
I am claiming back my pride that you put so much effort into taking from me
I am fighting for my identity that you left crippled and meaningless behind your expectations
And I attest that my confidence is only unappreciated by those who are fearful of it
I am transforming this battleground into your shooting range and I am no longer your target
You owe me nothing
You owe me nothing I understand that
Only you know the weight of the demons you fought off in order to have me here today
But I am still severely wounded by the things you choose to say
And I will no longer erase parts of myself to accommodate your rage

MUTINTA BBENKELE

# EDEN'S KNELL

I saw them come to tear the house
Bulldozer's teeth of fury's arrest
To witness my tears, to see me run,
I grabbed the kids
and said goodbye to Eden's lair.
Money's warmth, Love's menace ensnared.

I watched them slash my bedside lamp
Swirling shreds to labour's rust
Pictures dancing in the wind
Debris belching at my feet.

We saw the crystal shattered moon,
And walked away from Eden's knell
With Memory's blood and rubble's glaze.

We varnished our home with ashes
and stained our Love to dust.

TANISHA BHANA

# IN THE MOOD TO MONKEY

I am in the mood to go to the beach
with my whole family
and our neighbours.

I am in the mood to take my whole neighbourhood
    to the beach
with all our extended families
and their friends

You know what
I am in the mood to go to the beach with my whole
    neighbourhood
and their extended families
and their friends
and their extended families
and all their cows and their goats and their sheep and
    their huts.

In fact,
screw it;
let's slaughter at the beach.
Bring your cattle and poultry and let's have ourselves a
    good old funky "monkey" get-down party.
Sigide kuyoshona ilanga.[1]
I'm in the mood to go fishing for my ancestors who
    drowned as slaves
Whose bones are still weighed down by chains
I'm in the mood to make red the sands of every coast,
to erect monuments with the bones of our slaughtered
    cattle.

To fence off these oceans with fire.
To pollute the air with drums.
To loiter in our God-given waters.
To call forth the fallen with black-magic

I'm in the mood to chant …
in honour of my ancestors.
My forefathers.
My heroes.
My mother.
My children and theirs come.

I'm in the mood to "monkey."

       ZÉWANDE BK BHENGU

---

[1] We danced until the sun went down.

# KLEEDREPETISIE
*(foto's van ballet en #verset)*

Naby Nuweland dans 'n vuurkring mans
in stadige protes-pirhouette
om die klipvoete van
'n koloniale kalant
terwyl
Braamfonteinballerinas trippel
oor die blou plankmeer in 'n wit
swanesirkel

Op die voorblad van die oggendkoerant
wys die swart swaan se lang arm
elegant na die buiteband wat poelrond
brand –
kopieer toevallig op Sistynse-Kapel-trant
omgekeer 'n oomblik en 'n hand

Asof deur die vingers van 'n kindse
skilder vasgevang
pryk hierdie dubbelballet
op lamppale al langs
em | ma | ren | tia | dam

en ek probeer gister dekodeer,
kyk op na die duiwe die boeings
en stemme in die lug –
wil 'n beeld uit die baaierd voorkeer
maar geweld is vinniger as 'n gedig

RENE BOHNEN

# DRESS REHEARSAL
(*photos of ballet and #revolt*)

Close to Newlands a fire-circle of men
dance in slow protest-pirouette
around the stone feet of a
colonial chap
while
Braamfontein-ballerinas tripple
across the blue plank-lake in a white
circle of swans

On the front page of the morning paper
the black swan's long arm points
elegantly to the tyre burning pool-round –
accidentally copies à la Sistine Chapel
inversely a moment and a hand

As if captured through the fingers
of a senile painter
this double-ballet graces
the lampposts all along
em | ma | ren | tia | lake

and I try to decode yesterday,
look to the pigeons the boeings
and voices in the air –
attempt to salvage an image from the chaos
but violence is faster than a poem

*Translated from the Afrikaans original – Rene Bohnen's*
*'Kleedrepetisie' – by Pieter Odendaal*

# PIPE DREAM

Give us the good gospel, child in the street –
Broken bottle-neck prophecies;
Nyaope-laced philosophies ...
Wait a moment, for it to take you far away,
Up to the highest vantage point,
In your township squalor St Tropez.
Try if you can, to look through the blurry haze,
At the overturned buses, and tyres set ablaze.
The colonies have fallen; London Bridge is burning-
Join the youth who spit on Rhodes, but demand his higher
    learning.
Laugh at the vultures circling, vying for your vote,
Ignore the stench of carcasses, and skeletons rocking the
    proverbial boat.
Shake your head at their prodigal sons; despair that the
    true pioneers and beacons,
Have been swallowed whole by the depraved descent, and
    died out with the last Mohicans.[1]
The red berets' allure of communism has a shiny gleam,
But remember some men are more equal than others,
If even in just your pipe dream.

                          KATHRYN CLARE BOTES

---

[1] Mohicans in reference to the idea that the great leaders and examples heralded as pioneers and warriors of equality, social justice, etc., were the last of a dying breed.
Some men are more equal than others in reference to the famous Ambrose Bierce quote: "All men are created equal. Some, it appears, are created a little more equal than others."

# THE THIRST

Do you remember
Canada Dry
Coo-eee
And Amla
In all the colours

Do you remember
The milky
Delivering milk
In glass bottles
Before sunrise

Do you remember
Leaving plastic coupons
For guava juice
And fresh orange juice
Alongside the milk?

Do you remember the day
That he chased his whiskey
With milk
You bought
For the babies?

Do you remember
Trying to catch the words
Before they left your mouth
Do you remember
The look in his eyes?

Before he stood up
Before he grabbed
The glass milk bottle
Before he pulled you close
By your hair?

Do you remember
The look on your little girl's face
When she saw the blood
Do you remember the taste
In your mouth?

Do you remember
Telling the children
To step back
From the broken glass
While you picked up the pieces?

Do you remember being thirsty?

                DIANNE CASE

# REFUGEE

All day I walk the burning land,
at night the moon hides.
I sit in the belly of a rock
and breathe the mountain.
Secrets lurk in crevices trying to find God.

I'm a host of people walking in silence,
I'm a chattering of starlings.
It's the blindness of not knowing,
a ridge of flame in the distance,
my world paper burning at the edges.

All day I walk the burning land,
at night I listen to the dark,
talk into the spaces of what's left.
I hardly remember my dreams, my family
imagined like white chalk on the black canopy.

In the morning I rise again, pull my future.
Someone is lying cold in the broken bushes,
the whirring of blades,
the fire on the mountain, the days crying
an enamel bowl.

All day I walk the burning land,
the night a flat slab of stone.
I'm all these grains of sand, carried in a straight line.
Do I know this person, these drops of rain?
I can only allow it to trickle down my throat.

CHRISTINE COATES

# TERRA NULLIUS[1] – THE MARIKANA SYMPHONY

Do you hear the shouts of men, the creaking clanking mines
Do you see the empty land, this land that belongs to no one?
It's just a landscape, a land scope, a parcel, a portion;
the knobkerries beat the rhythm, the pangas, the sticks.
Do you hear the spinning wheels, the sounds at the edges, the beat of fists and feet?
This is the Marikana Symphony, the Marikana March.

Do you smell the dust of that hill, the sickle-shaped leaves,
bare land, crown land, rock rocking away?
Do you remember that April when we would be free,
when life was changing?
Since Sharpeville 52 years – ways of closing our eyes.
This is the Marikana March, the Marikana Symphony.

Do you see the colour of men telling stories
of treasures below the land, finders keepers,
where people are invisible, ways of forgetting.
It's the man of trees, he walks, he talks.
They're just paper words, they won't save you.
It's the beauty of terra nullius, it's the Marikana March.

Night is coming, papers blowing.
It comes on the wind, the rusted bushes, miners on random hills.
Can you hear their marching feet, the sound of sticks?
It's the Marikana Symphony.

Go wash your faces seven times, let the long knives fall,
these bullets won't harm you.

Do you see the colour of that day, the dust, the rock, the
 dried-out trees.
do you watch until it becomes a kind of blindness, report,
 retort?
It's dreamtime, time for rude awakenings.
It's a small koppie framing the story, marking,
lettering each murder site;
it's yellow stars painted on rock, dirt, dust, thorns.

It's the beauty of terra nullius, it's the Marikana March;
we've become what we most despised.
It's just a landscape, a land scope, a parcel, a portion.
Look in the dust, it's the empty land, land belongs to no
 one.
Night is coming. It's the night of terra nullius, it's the
 Marikana Symphony.

CHRISTINE COATES

---

[1] Terra nullius: In International Law terra nullius is territory that nobody owns so that the first nation to discover it is entitled to take it over, as in "finders keepers".

## "WINTER COLD"
*a spoken word poem*

It is winter cold
Outside a performance venue
When my white woman car
Chokes and splutters dead.

I am pale woman alone,
Winter cold
When soft hands black man
Answers my icicle tongued
"Please, help me."

He is winter cold
Black sweater on brown skin,
He smiles coffee cream warm and
Breathes life into engine dead.

Moments later,
My pale body is summer thaw
Driving breathing car,
Icicle tongue melting
To Lauryn Hill music playing
Down Jo'burg highway when –
Black man
Different black man;

Autumn leaf crumpled and brown boot clad
Is standing, shivering,
Winter cold, on the side of the road
Beside his car, engine dead,
Gesturing

"Please, help me."

I am pink woman.
Cheeks flaming carnation red
At black man in darkness
Who I've been taught to dread
Because black man in darkness
Rings sirens in white woman head
Because black man in darkness
Means headline could read
"White Woman Dead."

I am heat-wave shame.
Skin pulsing crimson, wilting carnation
Knuckles clutching guilt-white to steering wheel
Driving too fast from unfounded dread,
From black man asking for help,
Standing,
Winter cold,
Knees trembling on the side of the road
As I did,
As you have
Only to be neglected
By people like me
Wearing skin a lighter shade of "Please"
Speaking in a paler tone of "Help me."

BELLA (B-LYRICAL) COX

# CHOKING
*a spoken word poem*

To the sexist, republican, meat-eater
That sat next to me on my four-hour plane journey;
The flesh of the bodies you have killed with your appetite
Is stuck between your teeth.

I like to think that this,
Is a cow's last revenge.

You moved your mouth like a bulldozer
Your tongue; heavy and dense
Flattening any unruly arguments.
Upper lip rolling over tongue,
Bottom lip teeth chewing on.

I had to hold my nose when you spoke.

Biiiiig mouth.
Too big for your head.
You spoke like you swallowed;
Without mulling.

Your thoughts;
Regurgitated chunks
From other mouths akin to yours.
Too big.

Decades of bulldozer tongues in
Wide jaws and heavy set frames
Crushing those smaller ones
In your way.

Your eyes bulged.
Fear,
When I spoke.
They say the truth is hard to swallow,
Like over-cooked meat,
Tough.
Words like 'Feminism' got lodged in your throat.
A cat's hair ball.
I watched you ch- ch- choke.

My liberal views; swaying trees of freedom
A forest for you to demolish?
Doesn't your hatred get tiresome?

You claimed to enjoy a hearty conversation.
A debate rare till bloody,
A discussion of meat cleavers and hacksaws.
But
Your talks were uneven.

The carcass on the butchers table
Is already beaten and bleeding,
A fair fight for no one
Bulldozer butcher always winning,
This is how you function
Change course for no one.
But.
The flesh of my ideas got stuck between your teeth.
Stubborn woman.
Crazy ideas.

But I left your butcher's bulldozer table
Still walking,
Tongue still writhing,
Liberal views still swaying
Female brain still thinking

Leaving you,
To keep tooth picking
And truth
Choking.

                    BELLA (B-LYRICAL) COX

# ALL CHANGE

On the train today
a man offers me his seat
stands reading *South Africa Insight Guide*
the blind singer shuffles the carriage length
"God brings light to the world"
hopeful plastic cup in hand
as we rattle through Mowbray
a slender Cameroonian lady
shyly confides she is the daughter
of one of her father's four wives
and hides her big buck teeth
with her hand as she laughs
at Salt River an armless man
spits at the guard
when asked to show a ticket
blind singer shuffles the other way
"Light to Africa's children"
scramble off at Cape Town Central
all change here
around the unconnected computerised barriers
past the chewing gum ticket lady
skate across the faux marble concourse
into the glorious cacophony
dart between throbbing taxis
dive into the heat and colour of
my Africa.

LISE DAY

# THE ARCHBISHOP'S LAMENT

Eventually
they dismantled the rainbow,
colour by colour.

> GRAHAM DUKAS

# METAMORPHOSIS

More and more, I forget who it is I am asked to be.
And by the way, this is without the shame
of knowing who I am. Like it or not,
the apple does not fall that far from the tree.

A tree without leaves is the same tree with leaves;
only, it's waiting or has finished waiting,
or is dead, although that's not the point here.
I can't be both all the time – that's not how it is

in the world. The world itself seems to be waiting
or, if the signs of Spring are to be believed,
is tired of waiting. What happens next is without
pain or joy but is simply in the natural order

of things. I know that we are all rooted to the earth.
What keeps the elephant walking, is water –
not that which it drank this morning, but that which
it needs for tomorrow and the day after.

Could it be the same for me when I suggest
that we burrow into the earth and stay there?
Not for a whole year, but just long enough to allow
the trees to find their leaves and us our wings.

> GRAHAM DUKAS

# PLACE OF THE JACKAL

The sun beats down on Mapungubwe
red sun, red rocks, red sand.

Ah – my people
we remember green plains
of millet sorghum cotton.

We remember our king
rainmaker
sitting high on the hill with his court.

When death came to those high born
we buried them upright
packed round them
their glass, copper, gold
necklaces, ornaments, pots and plates,
objects of use in another world.

Elephants came to Mapungubwe
offered their tusks of ivory.

Rich earth showed us its treasures.

We were beloved of the gods.

Now the wind whines round Mapungubwe
graves of our fathers lie bare
bones scattered.

Place of jackals
but the jackals are gone.

Red rocks, red dust, red sun.

ELAINE EDWARDS

# IN RESPONSE TO SEEING AN AFRICAN WOMAN ABBA A DOG ON FACEBOOK

Black woman
your back rented out
to carry pups, babies
while yours cry at home.

Black woman
a blanket around
ancient bones,
symbol of care.

In its folds you fail
to hide your shame
as the camera greets you.

Black woman
wrought to pain
picturesque
unyielding.

No one sees you
or know your born name.

Black woman
Will they finally see you
when your back is broken?

          CONNIE FICK

# RE KWALA TSE DI SWA

Re kwala tse di swa ka ga rona
Re tokafatsa matshelo a rona
Re fodisa botlhoko jwa kgethololo
Re gata mebila ya poelano le borona
Re ipatlisisa mo leseding la kgololosego
Re tlhomamisa borona kgatlhanong le tsa maloba le
  maabane.
Re direlola dikgatlego tse di gatelelang bokgoni jwa rona
Re Afrika Borwa wa phetogo
Le fa bangwe ba re rogaka ka ntlha ya bontsho jwa mmala
  wa rona
Botsokunapi le borukhutlhi bo tshosetsa diphitlhelelo tsa
  setshaba
Ditsuatsue tsa phamokate kokwanatlhoko di tsubutla
Di batla go fedisa banna le basadi ba
  kamoso
Melelo e lakaila madirelo le dikolo nakong tsa megwanto
Thuto re e bone kae?
Botlhale le boitsaanape jwa thari e ntsho di agwa ke mang?
Ka dikgarooroo tsa Dikganetsano di ile magoletsa,
  boraadipolotiki ba kgotlhile motshitshi wa bogagapa.
Re tla leba kae ka
Le baeteledipele ba setshaba ba bolaelwa ditilo ka ntlha ya
  ditlhopo
Re tla botsa mang, fa e le rona re bolaanang?
A re aga re tla re thuba?
A re baakanya re tla re senya?
Re tla tshela leng toro ya katlego ya Afrika?
Afrika o tla tsoga leng go phitsimelwa le lesedi la
  kgololosego?

Re tla tsaya leng maikarabelo a bokamoso jwa ga Africa
 Borwa
Gore re kwakwante tsabakelong ya ditiro tsa rona tsa
 manontlhotlho
Re tshele ka tshepiso ya bokamoso jo bo edileng
Re bue ka Lentswe le lengwe gore re bafenyi
Barui
Babusi ba kgololosego
Ka re aparetswe ke lekhubu la phetogo go metsa lehuma la
 botlhokatiro
Go atlhamisa dikgoro tsa ditshono
Afrika Borwa wee
Motsala bagaka
Itlhokomele o sale moswa
Jaaka kgarebe e kgogedi
O sephutha ditshaba
Se wele ka lenga la seloko
Batsietsi ba ba ntsi
Bula matlho Pele ba go amoga lefatshe le humile ka
 meepo.
Gopola madi a badirameepong a tshologetseng lefela
Ao lebetse?
Se thanye lomapo lo le tsebeng
Pele ba go dira mmapereko
Mmaboithatelo
O mabontle
Jaaka setlhare fa thoko ga letsha o tlhomame.
Itshepe
O na le bokgoni
O kgakgatha ka tlhotlheletso

O shuma ka ditshono
Moremogolo ke wa taola
Wa motho wa ipetla
Dira matshetshe
O kgabile ka mmala wa sibilo
O setswerere sa botaki
Re kwala tse di swa ka ga rona.

    TSHEPO GAERUPE

# WE WRITE NEW ONES

We write new ones about ourselves
We better our lives
We remedy the pain of segregation
We also walk the path of reconciliation
We find ourselves in the glow of liberation
We humble ourselves against yesterday's bad situation
We undo what derails our abilities
We are a changing South Africa

Even when others insult us for our blackness

Violence and corruption threaten our nation

The cyclone of HIV/AIDS ravaging us
To destroy the future of both men and women

Fires destroy property and schools during protests
Where will we study?
How do we build wisdom and expertise of black people?

Violence of opposition is out of control, politicians are out of order

Where will we go
With community leaders killed for positions during elections

Who will we ask when it's us doing the killing?

When we build and demolish?

When we prepare and destroy?

When will the story of Africa's success be told
When will the light of liberation shine on you?
When will we take the responsibility for South Africa's tomorrow?

For us to walk proudly and celebrate or achievements
Give us hope for the future
Speak in one voice that we are winners
Wealthy
Rulers of freedom

We are exposed to the cloud of change to swallow unemployment
To open the gates of opportunities

Hail South Africa
Mother of heroes
You are still young take care of yourself
Like a maiden
You are a refuge
Don't change for the worst
Many will try to mislead you

Open your eyes before you lose your mineral-rich mines
Remember the blood of miners was shed in vain
Have you forgotten?

Listen to the good news
Lest they enslave you
Mother of what your own wishes

You are beautiful
Like a tree on the banks of a lake
Stand tall

You are gifted
You move with inspiration
You expose opportunities
The big tree is for remedies
A human tree sculptures itself

Do your thing
You are beautiful
You are a beacon of art
We are writing new stories about us

*Translated from the Setswana original – Tshepo Gaerupe's*
*'Re kwala tse di swa' – by Goodenough Mashego*

## HLAL' APH' EMZINI NGOB' IINKOMO ZIYATHETHA

Hlal' aph' emzini
Ngob' iinkomo ziyathetha!
Ndamamela endiyal' umama
Ndingayaz' ukuba uqum' inyala

Wathi kum, ntombi yam
Sana lwam
Yazi
Lisemzini ingcwaba lomfazi

Nyanga nenyanga
Ndaboph' inyanda
Ndisebenzela abantwana bam
Kuba lo umthwalo ngowam

Ingaba ezinkomo zithini xa zithetha?

Zithi, mandinyamezele ukuthwala izandl' entloko
Kuba undibetha oko?
Zithi, mhla nezolo mandikhale isijwili
Ndilale intliziyo ilihlwili?

Ndiziva ndikhumbul' emva
Nda kujonga phambili limfilib' ikamva
Ndicand' amathafa
Ndoyik' ukufa

Ndilivile ilizwi leenkomo
Iinyembezi zinqamlez' umbombo
Ndanyamezela
De umphefumlo wanikezela

Inene ingcwaba lomfazi lisemzini

Hlal' aph' emzini ngob' iinkomo ziyathetha!

    NOBUNTU GANTANA

# STAY IN YOUR MARITAL HOME, FOR CATTLE SPEAKS VOLUMES

Stay in your marital home,
for cattle speaks volumes!
I obeyed my mother's instructions
Unaware that she was burying a shame

She spoke to me; she said,
Dearest daughter,
Know this:
A married woman's grave
Is in her marital home

Month after month
I fastened my lot
Labouring for my children's sake
This burden was mine alone to carry

What would these cows say, were they to speak?

Would they say I should endure your beatings

And throw my hands above my head in despair?
That I should cry my lungs out daily
And sleep with a broken heart each night?

I am engulfed by reminiscence
For my future seems blurry
As I traverse many a hill
In fear of my own death

I heard the cow's voice
As tears formed a crucifix across my nose bridge
And I persevered
Until my soul admitted defeat

A married woman's grave
is indeed in her marital home

Stay in your marital home,
For cattle carries speaks volumes!

*Translated from the isiXhosa original – Nobuntu Gantana's*
*'Hlal' aph' emzini ngob' iinkomo ziyathetha' –*
*by Vuyokazi Ngemntu*

# DRAGONS AND FLAMES

We should start fires in the mines
Flames flying along tunnel after tunnel

Our miners will become dragons
Hundreds of thousands of them

They will fly with flames along the tunnels
Their breaths burning the dark that eats them

Our dragon-miners with fire breaths,
Fire wings, take their place in the destruction
That has haunted their lives in underground mouths

The fires that this land has been aching for
Screaming along its belly, exploding
All the unspoken scars that are
Constantly used to decorate flags

All the screams, silences,
Stuffed into pots to produce the gold coins
To feed the empty mouth at the end of the rainbow

We need to stop pretending
Stop trying to walk while disappearing

We will start fires in the mines,
The flames will eat the tunnels in a roar
If we listen closely we will hear our new
National anthem in the flames

Our miners will burst into dragons
Immortal

Taking all their children onto their wings
As they explode out the mine shafts
So their children
And the children of the miners who died before
They grew wings

Can watch the mines explode
Unable to escape being consumed by light
Can hear the dragons, and the flames,
Can hear the children and the ghosts
Can hear us sing.

SARAH GODSELL

# MOTHER AND DAUGHTER WALK

in the stage four cancer ward
you tell me you see your mother walk
towards you in her hair-down-to-buttocks days.
vital in the lilt of her step,
her dress summer swinging,
her blood pulsing like a strobe light.

you step together round a lake
that stretches both your strides.
feet skipping like stones
skimming the surface.
the swan of a smile, the grin of a goose
an exhalation of larks keep you company.

once again she is origin.
then she pushed you out in a
cord-cutting moment. now she gathers
you in, welcomes you in your prime,
all ageing shed into the lake,
to a world beyond the first womb.

                            DORIAN HAARHOFF

# FATHER AND SON SONG

I sing of father gone and son's loss,
of the range and ridges that divide them
in sheer rise, the pass iced, the path overgrown,
of oceans, deserts and cities that split them.

fathers roaring from the touch line
egging on the son to become a
better-stronger-faster-famous-unlived him,
stuffing his son into his empty sports socks.

the man who hangs a sign above the shop front
Father and Son Pty Ltd, forcing the boy
into a trade, a profession not of his choosing
to plod his footsteps in shoes too small.

a father who punches sons and their mothers,
neither who reach up to his armpit,
whose combined weight does not scale his.
who repeats the fist and strap he witnessed.

one whose heart stopped mid-sentence,
the boy falling back into his mother's nest
in long featherless adolescence,
trapped as man of the house.

I sing of another father I saw sprawled
across a mid-morning bed, unmade,
who swam within the brandy barrel,
his life diving bottomless into binge lake.

the gone-to-war man in the distance
who falls from the air, in the desert storm
or returns with night horrors of ripped limb raids,
screaming the dreams he never speaks of.

a father who teaches stoic robot emotion
stiff lip, square shoulder, erect spine
then leaves the youth to face his mother's rage
while he directs the boardroom traffic.

I sing too of father found and son growing.
that rare breed, wild yet bridled, the prodigal dad
who reads his off spring like a love sonnet,
stories him in his own truth, wonders at the marvel
   of his loins.

that dad who travels, yes, away, yet daily expresses
in the visible and invisible, his gut laugh and praise.
walks in the boy's company in love of the double helix
and the *viva la difference* mystery of sperm. I sing I sing.

DORIAN HAARHOFF

# FLESH AND BONE TANGO

in an African origin myth
people came forth from a tree.
the sculptor calls his creation,
placed in a museum, man and skeleton.

hewed from the same stump
these two figures in the carving
lean away from each other
where the trunk splits into a V.

he has trapped them
in a still moment, turning a dance,
joined below the hip.
the man, alert, watches the skull,

wary lest it edges nearer
playing it rib cage concertina,
exhaling, exhaling, clasping him
in a lover's tangle.

                        DORIAN HAARHOFF

# COMING HOME

I remember the journey. Two days of driving.
Postcards replicating in my rear-view mirror.
Ahead the horizon flat and clouds
I never seemed to reach.
The grey-black road ululated beneath me.
Hands cramped. Clenched. Unclenched.
Blisters formed. Calluses immature
from years of catching trains.

The voices at petrol stations *Goeie More*
and food stops *Kea Leboha*[1]
spoke in unfamiliar languages *Hamba kahle*.[2]
Replies hesitated and twisted off my tongue *Molo,
    Unjani?*[3]
I had to relearn the sounds of this land.

And then on the last afternoon – driving
through a green valley, mountains
guarding the landscape – I felt the roads
closing behind me. The long Huguenot Tunnel
spat me out into a hot dusty basin –
air fogged, reeking.

But this was years ago, years.
It doesn't seem worth talking about now
the hope and sunshine that
towed me home.

On wind punched afternoons
when the rain drives in cold –
and the constant view of Table Mountain
becomes disorienting –
I remember everything I left behind.

### KERRY HAMMERTON

---

[1] Thank you
[2] Go well
[3] Hello, how are you?

# X-MAS TIDE

By proclamation – Ring the holly!
Tell the nation to be jolly.
Invade their minds with tapes of jingle bells
Come by! Come buy! The profit-margin swells.
Buy three, one free! That's more for me.
Parcels pile up in the hall. Have we got a gift for all?

In the townships, fire spreads through the tin shacks
Leaving thousands in desperation, only blacks.
Men mourn beside their dead
Jobless, homeless, unfed.
Over-filled rubbish-bins stink
With over-indulgence and no time to think.

JAY HEALE

# ABA TE (CARRY ME)

Carry me
through the streets of //Hui !Gaeb.
Aba te!
into the Alibaba cave of forgotten treasures
underneath the tar the ground cautions with blood mixed
    between us
Aba Te!
passed seats of parliament fattened with gluttons who sell
righteous tales to full pockets and vandalise a constitution
    for personal gain

I hunger
Corrugated iron arts the landscapes with misery
airports trudge tourists in //Hui !Gaeb streets
to hear more lies and lay their bodies on beds in hotels
owned by outlanders and rich land thieves
whose children upgrade places that still echo the sounds
    of children born in mutilated colours
and call it gentrification
old lies
some of us forget and assimilate
"You let them cut out your tongue and make an unmarked
    grave for it!"
the clock ticks and time does not heal

Aba Te! a revolution
cry me a river
even now when you say "sorry"
the roof still leaks
my people still sleep in the doorways of city streets

and new governments tilt on old foundations manned by
    the cogs of old machines
in these foundations are the bones of dreams turned night

Aba Te!!
A recollection of five Dutch/Khoe wars
resistance never spoken in museum mouths
divide and rule simmers on stoves in kitchens
the 'us and them' parodying itself into new formed
    histories
poison food for the stomachs of babes

Aba Te!
fetch me back Diana like you did Sarah Baartman
from the country of my dispossession
show me the unmarked grave of my tongue there where
boegoe still grows in Khoekhoegowab
where Hoerikwaggo still makes love with the sky in
    Khoekhoegowab
my blood and yours in Khoekhoegowab
dagga, karree
gogga en kierie
geitjie en kwagga in Khoekhoegowab
praat vannie 'kamma' unity in diversity wat nog innie bek
    van divide en rule sit
en die 'eina' denial diep in my onbestaan
Wat pla en raas
Aba Te!

West where the coast meets Chocoqua
Aba Te!
ChariGuriqua
To the river Berg
Aba Te!
Across five star VOC scars

from the lips of Ethiopia to the hips of //Hui !Gaeb
that consonant Ɵ passed from North to South
to motherless vowels and syntax
Aba Te!
as my unfluent tongue spells names it never learned
into ears that never hear
because Khoekhoegowab still echoes on Hoerikwaggo's throne
and all along this Southern African deep the plants and animals
still steep their roots and hooves in Khoekhoegowab's keep.

TRACEY (KHADIJA) HEEGER

## SLOW COOKER

a pressured, cooked family
weakened by too much seasoning
close, strongly fragranced
ready to split in the heat, merging
into a soup of nothingness
well prepared, sliced and quartered
peeled open, gutted
mixed and slowly saturated
on a chestnut Autumn afternoon.

HEIDI ELISABETH HENNING

# PEOPLE OF THE SKY

We are of a different kind
For you to understand poems, people have to die
We play house in broken homes
We praise God with burdened hearts
We fill our pockets with stones to weather the storm

Belly buttons are navigators to eve's garden
A stomach of a rich man is a haunting memory to a
    starving child
The sight of a toothpick is a reminder of the reality he left
    back home

People of the sky

The tides have turned
Rain is coming from the soil
Pilchards have drank the oceans dry
Dolphins have found solace on mountain peaks
Summer days are colder than ever
Trees are holding oxygen hostage
Human beings are keeping carbon dioxide for themselves
The bartering system is crumbling
Looking at the stars …
Please hear my prayers, it's bad out here

People of the sky

Hurricanes are keeping children safe from their so-called
    fathers
Racism is now the seventh wonder

Scars are symbols of peace between lovers
Pyramid schemes are now schematics of sky scrappers
Nations are giving each other bombs as presents
Graves have become homes for the living
Cigarettes are chilling in passage ways smoking humans to kill time

People of the sky ...
I hope my prayers are not falling on deaf ears.

Now I remember this time, we have been here before
A time where if you want to give these people hope? Give them vengeance
A time were we have more statues of rhinos than we have living ones
Technology has taken over
Handwritings are becoming extinct
Hashtags have become substitute for burning tyres
Too many a people die in the name of Jesus
A man?
But sometimes they forget that corpses never made a good foundation
And in this house? The only commandment they need to follow is mine
Where the best way through a man's heart is to crack open his ribs
But not every treasure chest contains all that is glittery
Sometimes your worst nightmares are buried in there
Those we loved are now in boxes we do not want to claim
I pledge my legions to those who graduated in obituaries

For university degrees are only for the privileged few
Religion has become an expensive commodity
Money is asking people for change
Even though we tithe till our spines collide
People of the sky
I've had enough victims for the night
I'm going back to where it all started
Where blind men were still fortune tellers.

THAPELO HLONGWANE

# MAMBHELE'S HARVEST

My grandmother was a guardian,
Tending a kingdom of cabbages.
Leafy, layered planets in constant orbit emasimini.
UmamBhele was a general, rearing
A battalion for survival at 50 cents a head.
In imitation of Genesis,
She could sculpt a field into her image
Before the sun had sobered to rise.

Her husband, uNcotshe, was himself a spade –
Toiling in the tunnels of Jozi – the colon of Gauteng;
Constipated with gold. And the bodies of black men.
Spewing them out on opposite ends:

One to the baas. The other to the grave.

My grandfather was an intercessory prayer
Praying in picks. Penance paid inside a rock –
His sweat would flow from the mines
Like rivers. Like letters. Like sacrifice and provision.
Sometimes like signals of smoke. All the
Way to Keiskammahoek, then funnelled
into grandmother's veins of steel,
With a back as broad as the mountains of uQoboqobo.
She would midwife a harvest, all … Canaan-like. All …
    giant heads and paradise-like.

This cabbage connoisseur
Could craft seven variations of cabbage dishes;
Each layer its own revelation until

There was a testimony between
Those leaves –

Umakhulu noTamkhulu ngabantu bomhlaba.
And my inheritance is in the land under my fingernails.
So when it rains, I crave the soil … three times a day.
Some call it anaemia. But
I know it to be communion.

Mother was born a pillar of soil
With tendrils for fingers, even now the plants at home
    gravitate towards her as if
She is the sun.
Setting into the room.

Perhaps they are descendants of cabbages packed solar
    system tight
on Saturday mornings
On the back of ibakkie yakwa Mampinga:
Where grandmother's soldiers
rattled along to town against the backtrack of
an exhaust pipe. Harmonising,
"50 cents! 50 cents amakhaphetshuuuu!
2 for R1!"

At school she must study Agriculture. In Afrikaans.
This mother of mine who swings a hoe in cursive
– with more finesse than a pencil –
Who learned the cradle of land
From the canyons in her parents' hands,

The daughter of a miner,
And a village farmer.
must learn the only thing she understands, In a language her tongue
does
not.

1984
Grandfather's body turns to gold. Six feet deep. He will not be mined.

1992
John Voster Primere Skool.
The second black in an Afrikaans school
– all dolled up in white and blue –
A definite sign of a South Africa new.
Juffrou reads out the register and non-existent clicks intimidate her ...
Sifokazi Jonas?
Sifo – disease. Kazi – big.
Ladies and gentleman I am now, Big Disease Jonas!
Here ma'am ... My father will explain.

1995
White and blue with added red: English schools are the new means to an end
So we pilgrimage to a multiracial res.
On introduction night our names sit on our tongues like trays.
– Flashback – "Sifokazi Jonas."

Maybe a twang is the antidote? Hi, my name is
    Siphowkarzy Jonas.
Laughter rolls off the other trays:
She's trying to be white.

1999
My sister is a new recruit to this post-TRC world where
the search for a better life means
School mornings on the back of Oom Koos' red
botsotso bakkie. As red
as our school ties.
Nathi singamakhaphetshu. We are also cabbages. Two for
    R1!

2001
Grandmother is planted. Six feet deep. She will not be
    harvested.

Now
My mother is proud of how finely I chop cabbages;
The care I take in disassembling planets.

                              SIPHOKAZI JONAS

# WEEKLY SERVICE

MaDlamini is a church woman.
Decked in an Easter-bright blouse that never bleeds into
other clothes in the washing.
Her hat, the colour of Isaiah 1:8,
(and the forgiveness of sins)
peels naartjie-skin air with its axe-sharp pleats.
And the midnight sky draped around her hips
is deep, devoid of lint constellations.
There are no tears in her stockings. She is a lady.
Even when Methodist bells peal into a frost-infested
    Sunday morning –
she marches along, a misty apparition:
in red, white, black, like a dismantled vernacular bible;
A township epistle.

This weekend, pastor will preaches forgiveness –
Seventy times seven times.
But the burning-heart Jesus behind him speaks a sermon
    of his own.
That watered-down Oros messiah
with GHD hair;
the "get over it it's been 22 years already saviour."
That's madam's liberal "jesus". Born in Bethelehem, Free
    State.

MaDlamini knows that dinner table gospel,
the one that curses Liverpool and firepools, but never
    laments how
shacks, like sacrificial lambs, fall to a South-Easter ghoul.
Only how the dumping grounds of zinc depreciate the view.

Madam's son is the bishop of this religion –
In his third year at UCT.
The architecture of his bones is crafted in MaDlamini's milk.
He has been constructed by Xhosa lessons in the backyard,
and strolls along Claremont's songololo streets –
the ones that are still leaving history on a hundred legs –

This boy who shredded his tongue to pronounce udla in Dlamini
So he could ask to 'dla', ukudlala.
This boy who now calls her a girl …
or Doris.

Wednesday nights he breaks bread,
A communion that shuns BEE but harvests the honey.
The boy she hid-and-sought behind curtains and lace
scribes new scriptures: "These people must know their place!"
A place somewhere between 'amen' and washing a grown man's underwear.

MaDlamini goes to church seven days a week.
One day in heaven. The other six in hell.

On the side of her all-in-one room,
Her children wonder whether Mother Mary,
the patron saint of domestics,
has enough room for children who must bring

themselves up
by the teeth.
Who breastfeed frugally because mother's breast is on
 lease,
Who cannot shake the taste of a baby bishop in nappies.
This is their nativity scene.

Sunday pastor preaches Provision.
And calloused-hand, manager-born, fish- and bread-
 multiplying Messiah.
Maybe that Jesus can raise the children.

SIPHOKAZI JONAS

# I AM BEAUTIFUL

I am Beautiful
From the calloused feet that trudges the tired Earth
To the ends of my hair
Split from grooming and frivolity

I am Beautiful
From the pointed tips of my breasts
To the sagging of them under the weight
Of suckling young and egregious gravity

I am Beautiful
From the gnarled nails
That toiled the soil
Caressed your torso
To the dryness of my skin
That maps the world of my journeys

I am Beautiful
From the overhanging layers of my waist
That bore the burgeoning of pregnancy
To the sacred lines of my belly
That stretched and blossomed under the weight of life

I am Beautiful
From the fine lines that etch my face
To the curtain behind my eyes
From the equator of my lips
To the tropic of my jawline
I am Beautiful
From the taught beauty of youth

To the wrinkled crevices of ageing
Each line and wrinkle a milestone
In the mountain and mole hills of Life

I am Beautiful
From the swaying gait of my curvaceous derriere
To the lilting swagger of my rounded hips
I am Beautiful?
I am Beautiful!

        FIONA KHAN

# CLASS

There are lines drawn to separate the rich
from the poor. There are borders of class
everywhere. Lines running through towns.
It's only now that I notice them.
Because a payslip not only classifies you
but opens your eyes as well.

There are shops normally located near taxi ranks.
Shops where prices agree with a lifestyle
of not affording wheels.
There are tables of vendors all over taxi ranks.
Mothers wake up at dawn to sell fruits.
You only find them here.
Because no one emerges from a Mercedes
to buy from these tables –

deep inside the mall or near parking lots,
there are shops for such people.
Classy shops- unlike taxi ranks, unlike the township.
Shops more like suburbs.
You can't push a trolley from them to the public taxis.
They are too far.
This distance is what keeps you in place.
This distance reminds you where you belong.

                    MUSAWENKOSI KHANYILE

# CHURCH

I've done many stupid things in the name of love
but today I'm wearing a white shirt
and sharp-pointed shoes.
My girlfriend, who invited me here,
winks at me before taking a seat
in the ladies' section.

(some churches are as gender sensitive
as toilets).

The service proceeds into something
I've seen on television before.
People sing joyously.
A few jump around in front
leading choruses.

As a boy I used to walk with my dad to church.
Outside the township, in a shack
we connected with the heavens.
Today I'm the prodigal son
who's returned to a revamped home.

The pastor reads out the scripture
from his tablet.
His tongue sails along a number of accents,
borrowing tongues from countries over the seas.
A young man rises with a decorated basket
for offerings.
The speed point machine appears

to my now widened eyes.
Cards are being swiped in front
while others throw notes in the basket
singing about a Jesus who died for them
on the cross.

It seems I've been away for a very long time.
It seems that way.
I glance around like a stranger
taking everything in.
Church used to be familiar home.

## MUSAWENKOSI KHANYILE

# OMRING

ek klim die heuwel agter ons huis uit
'n kille wintersoggend in lidgetton, die midlands van
    kwazulu-natal
'n wilde wind terg my ywerige enkels en kuite
met jagende asems kom ek bo
ek kyk uit vir die plaat klippe
waarop ek my gedigte gaan voordra

skielik breek twee rietbokke die stilte
en snel pylend oor die vlaktes
al agter hulle ratse pote slaan
swart koolstof op uit die gebrande gras
met 'n goeie afstand tussen ons
gaan staan hulle stil en kyk my stip aan
hulle vertrou nie die vrede nie
en deins vlugtig uit my sig

ek vind my verhoog van klippe
en begin my gedigte een na die ander opsê
ek herhaal oor en oor die lyne van my gunsteling vers
*hoe dig 'n mens vanuit die denklose plek*
*daar waar dit net suiwer, spontane metafoor is*
*wat roekeloos uit die keelgat lek*
*en in filigraan lettergrepe*
*stalaktieties in oorbuise drup*

ek voel aan dat iemand na my luister
ek kyk gedurig om my heen
dit is net gras, wind en heuwels
ek is nie alleen

ek voel die land se bloed, vesels,
kleure, liedere,
tonge en velle
voor my opdoem
daar is stemme in die wind
ek wil glo dat die asems van
my voorvadergeeste
al om my waai
en uitbundig my keelklanke toejuig

        LARA KIRSTEN

# ENCIRCLING

I climb the hill outside our house
a chilly winter's morning in lidgetton, the midlands of
    kwazulu-natal
a wild wind teasing my industrious ankles and calves
with chasing breath I reach the top
I search for the stone slab
where I'll perform my poems

suddenly two reedbucks break the silence
speedily bolting across the plains
at their agile feet black charcoal
shoots up from the burnt grass
keeping a good distance between us
they halt and fix their eyes on me
they don't trust the peace
and quickly recoil from sight

I find my stage of rocks
and start reciting my poems one after the other
I repeat again and again the lines of my favourite poem
how does one write from this thoughtless place
there were all is pure, spontaneous metaphor
recklessly leaking from the gullet
and in filigree syllables stalactitically
dripping into earducts

I can sense someone listening to me
I look around incessantly -
only grass, wind and hills
I am not alone

I feel the blood of the land, its vessels,
colours, songs,
tongues and skins
rise up before me
there are voices in the wind
I want to believe that the breaths of
my ancestors
are fluttering all around me
thunderously applauding the sounds from my throat

*Translated from the Afrikaans original – Lara Kirsten's
'Omring' – by Pieter Odendaal*

# RIBBONS ON THE FENCE

Caught on the barbs of the fence
that separates the forest from suburbia
ribbons flutter.
Red for the blood spilt
on the scuffed pine needles
and the sand
where they forced her down;
white for the innocence
that took her running among the trees
for the pleasure of it;
green for her trustfulness
as they came towards her;
blue for the sea she surfed;
pink for loving friendship;
yellow for her happiness
and the sun shafting through the branches;
purple for mourning
without end.
No black ribbon shivers in the breeze
to remind us of the evil
in her murderers' minds
and the *tik* that turned their hearts
to cold coals.

LYNNE KLOOT

# NTSO YAMATHILE

Sekukade ndiziqhekeza ubuchopho ngawe

Ndizibuza imibuzo engenampendulo
Maxa wambi ndizibone ndiyimbangi
Kodwa ngaphakathi ndiyazi andonanga
Siyaphila esam isazela asifanga

Ndiyafunga yhini sithandwa
Amazulu angandingqinela
Esithi mna ndimsulwa
Kuba wena woyiswe kukuziphatha
Nguwe imbangela nguwe

Sobabini thina siyazi
Ukuba intliziyo inde
Wena kaloku awoneli
Nob'ubani angathini
Kodwa kambe wena waba nesikrokro
Kuba wena awoneli

Ungakhomba mna andikhathali

Emininzi ijolise kuwe awusaboni

Namatiletile ndiwenzile
Silungis'okungalunganga
Kodwa ezakho zibuthuntu

Andizisoli nakanye sithandwa sam
Kuba mna nawe siyazi
Zimsulw'izandla zam
Ixolil'eyam intliziyo
Hamba sithandwa sam hamba

NOMNIKELO KOMANISI

# KIDNEY OF THE SO-AND-SO CLAN

For a while now, I've wrecked my brain on your account,
Asking myself unanswerable questions.
At times I see myself as blameworthy
Though I know well that I am free of guilt
My conscience is at ease,
As one who has not erred.
I swear, my beloved one,
the heavens above can attest to my innocence
For it is you who failed to preserve your dignity.
You are to blame, yes you.
We both know
how insatiable the heart is,
Yours is most rapacious
Despite any efforts to please you
You remain ever doubtful
And yet harder still to please.
Point (all blame) at me, if you will
I don't care
Oblivious to how the rest of your fingers point towards
 you.
Great efforts have I made
That peace between us may be restored
Yet your ears remain hardened.
I haven't the slightest regret, my dear,
For in truth we both do know
That my heart is at peace
Go then, love – farewell!

*Translated from the isXhosa original – Nomnikelo Komanisi's*
*'Ntso yamathile' – by Vuyokazi Ngemntu*

# THERE'S A ME THAT'S STILL NOT FREE

Years into democracy she still belongs to a Bantustan,
This time bordered in the confines of her womanhood.
Her mind regarded half a mind - not fit to lead a country;
To lead a people she carried in her womb.
She's not a starter of wars
Nor is she a greedy belly ever consuming alone what is meant to be shared
But that's a strength and not a weakness

There's a me that's still, like the bird of Maya, caged
Caged and singing with a fearful trill the song of freedom
She sings the anthem and lifts the flag but with sluggish arms
How could she otherwise when last night she held in her arms the corpse of her neighbor
Who was slayed for loving another woman?
If we are not free to love who we love then which freedom are you singing about?

There's a me that's still very much the face of poverty
Still the fetcher of metaphoric firewood and water
Still a soft cushion for drunk husbands, a fur to ascertain manhood
There's a me that's still very much a punching bag for hungover boys who think themselves men
The slaps, the beating and battering I cover with make-up
Because I, like my grandmothers and their grandmothers
    I'm not allowed to speak freely about his abuse
Without being asked "What did you do to provoke him?"
Well, what did I do except be a woman?

There's a me who goes to school
The same school fathers send their ill-trained sons
Who will ascertain their manhood at any cost;
Planting in my belly continents that'll be filled with yet
    another loathed child
His mother says the fault is mine
For wearing a short skirt
His father says the fault is mine
For smiling suggestive
I say there's no fault except that I'm a woman

There's a me that's still not free
A me who still gets left at the door on the way to the
    boardroom
A piece of me that makes it in after a long race
Only to be spared a sorry seat
Because my melanin is, like the rest of my womanhood
    not good enough
Full of flaws that need rectification

There's a me who is not Eve,
But she is in every terrible way receiving Adam's revenge
A garden, a snake and a fruit;
One who looked like me gave Adam a fruit
And the judgement still beats my womb and breast.
But how long
How long will it remain the woman's fault?

                              PORTIA MABASO

# MOTHERS WARN YOUR DAUGHTERS

Dear lover
This is the fault found in you;
That you're the temple from which I say all my prayers
That God dared appear to me through you.
When you chose to be a window
Didn't you know it was forbidden to be stained?
That stones will crack you down?

When you chose to be the gate
From which love enters in
And a door from which she applies her balm
Didn't you know there was a fire kindled for you?
That you could burn to ashes?
Someone should have warned you that this is no place for
    feeble little girls.

Creeds have found you guilty
You have not met up to their laws
And they who didn't make you and therefore do not
    understand you have you standing on judgement.
Behold Nebuchadnezzar
Behold a burning furnace
Will you defend yourself?
Or do you choose to test the fury of his fire?
If you choose the fire and think yourself a Daniel
It best be that you have been fasting.
If it is fire you choose then here I am
Your faithful Shadrach

Here I am standing with you
Here I am loving you.
Here I am not deterring!

PORTIA MABASO

# HIP HOP

emotional bruises sting
for gutted youth
in a manufactured world
serving its own agenda.

we are wrung people
as empty as beer bottles
with silent fathers
who never took an interest in us.

people in a big hurry
the world drifting from us
we surrendered
to the shelter hip hop gave.

where songs hammered in the night
as we drank and smoked
in hip hop clubs
rising above the graves the world gave.

        SONGEZIWE MAHLANGU

# APARTHEID IN THE SKY

There is a world up in the stars
Far beyond Jupiter and Mars.
At that incredible height
You'd never guess, there was Apartheid

For those, whose Souls are white
Can live in Heaven here.
And Souls, with the blackness of the night,
Must be in Hell down there.

And Souls with colours in between
Must live in Purgatory, till they are white and clean

PATRICK MAITLAND

# THEY CAME

The plain was flat, wild, and desolate
They came when I, a San, was digging up a root.
There were three
They were brown Xhosa, bigger than me.
Though they spoke in a tongue I did not know
I knew that I had to go
Further South across the river

They came as I, a Xhosa, was working in the field
There were three
Tall black Zulu, with assegai and shield
And though they spoke in a language I did not know
They made me understand that I must go
With them to hear their chief
Say that my land was his.
But I may live in peace
If I went to another land, another place.

They came when I, a Zulu, was in my hut
They did not knock, though the door was shut
There were three
They were white, smaller than me
But they had guns which could kill
If I did not bend to their will
Though they spoke in a tongue I did not know
I knew I had to go
Further North across the river

They came when I, a white, was on my farm
They said they would do no harm

There were three
They were black, with paper and pen
They said they were here before me
And I must restore the farm to them
They knew it would hurt me so
But I had to go.

They came when I, a black, repossessed my land
There were three
The Ghosts of the San
They said because I was black I could remain
As long as I did not claim
The land of the San had always been mine.
If I lived in peace
And erased the hatred in my heart
I could start afresh
And find happiness.

PATRICK MAITLAND

# SALUTE TO KLIPSPRUIT RIVER
*25 November 1995*

May I your honour
Call you K!
Home-grown lingo of the closeness of family
That's how close we've grown together
To give our siblings space to think of lineage
To know indeed you are my "khazi" (cousin)
You gave life to me and those before us
Go on surprise us with your meandering metamorphic
    ageless face
Through boulders and klippe.

Somewhere in your meanderings
Sojourners erected townships
Semi refugee camps
And named one after you
Klipspruit
Kliptown
Names that could have stemmed seemingly
From a useless stream some thought
They gave their abodes names pregnant with freedom
    imaginings and Charters
You stream across deserted no man's lands
Clustered by shacks and shanty towns
Mekhukhu galore!
By your permission we stay
See just how we take pride in you
Klipsruit River!

Glimmer where there never was
Blessings seen over and over

Multiple untold truths you harbour
Till you are angered to the brim
And flood
And spew it all out
Truth
No lies
Till we pray your gods
The thunderstorms must stop!

Teachers do not always have to speak
Some do it by watching
Giving confidence to those who try things
Now we see the wisdom of your murmuring meanderings
Across the love of those who live on your banks
Banking their hopes on another day
A source of life to those in need
Washing!
Drinking!
Bathing!
Baptizing!

First there was the spirit
Some fool confused called it spruit
Magic creation at work
Remnants of world creation
That's how amakholwa nezinyanga
Responding to seeming calls of irreconcilable spirits
Zamadlozi noYesu perhaps dancing the dance of peace
In a world we mortals cannot fathom
Cross-carriers chanting in tongues of prophets before them

Bangoma calling ancestors gone
All known to the wisdom of your endless stream
Now we see the thunder and the kindness of your
    blessings
That goes namathongo
And those who dare call themselves
Bana ba Modimo alone
Klipspruit River!

Mothers we know
Care about those little things
In the faces of their children
Things that give them pride
Is this not what you ask of us
To respect your life-giving magic
Turned into a thousand faces
Trees and grass the shapeliness of nature
Free of debris
Free of beer cans
Free of petrol cans
Free of carcasses of dogs
Scraps and rubbish
Or someone's dead body
Or what – have - you
The very things that spoil your beauty
Our lifeblood
That's how we must let you be
If we tomorrow must live on.

Snake on
Wind on
Meander on
Till you reach Lekoa
Where you also must tonight rest we believe
Phila kade koze nathi siphile
Klipsruit River!

                MAISHE MAPONYA

# THE TRC – ON THE BOX
*22 April 1996*

I heard this story on the box
sitting in my match-box-shape house
about how truth must be told
and men and women sitting to listen
and perpetrators and victims spewing it out
tears and guts to speak of stories hidden and unknown
to earn a forgiveness
the dusk hour of seven had just struck.

This story blows my mind
never inclined to reconcile agony or torture with peace
despicable acts told
before men and women seeking to close the old chapter
imploring perpetrators to tell all
bang! Cradock four permanently removed from society
your wives my comrades
must give a wail today
Fort Calata
Matthew Goniwe
Sparrow Mkhonto
Sicelo Mhlauli
mutilations – mutilations – mutilations
how must a nation forgive
their wailings are proper.

Again and again the commissioners returned
the perpetrators too returned
they cried with the victims
for the sake of an imagined miracle
we're implored to forgive

how we lost husbands – wives – children
those dear to us
limbs preserved in bottles
grotesque museum pieces
the world would never have known
rainbow nation compromise
child of the "Sunset Clause"

What makes telling truth suddenly strange?
Saartjie Baartman relived in strange South Africa
fighting for world's first rainbow nation
TRC my foot!

These are not fireside stories
television is the modern brazier
producers and politicians choose to play the theory of odd
    museum games
I see the games in the museum box tonight
somewhere between seven and seven
wonders of charcoal nights
in the-age-of-the-computer-virus
being able to tell unimaginable stories
that we see and witness all on the box
truth commission commissioned at the table of
    compromise.

What makes telling truth suddenly strange?

How finally the victims go home
worse than they ever were

emotionally drained
tear-wells virtual deserts
evenings never failing in their rituals
to-make-a-happy-nation
these victims must make this nation happy
for the rainbw nation's peace.

Perpetrators are aplenty
They come and tell commissioners
not the peoples courts
how they did it
reliving their grotesque misdeeds
saying they were messengers of the system
today they trade crocodile tears for pardon
so commissioners can pity them
and they cry too
I had no more tears
while the bishop-on-the-chair prays for us all in the name
    of reconciliation
where did we come from by the way?

This nation can't just be yet.

And children of those who did it watch it
listening to how lethal syringes of Dr Death silenced "the
    enemy"
and victims and their children watch the box too
listening to how bodies of loved ones strapped to aircrafts
    were dumped into the ocean
clutched together in protective embraces

shock death squads' confessions are unbearable
the commissioners are the only ones going to the bank
for facilitating a job well done
for rainbow nation's sake
this, the poet cannot take.

In the small hours of the replay of history on the box
fatigue beckons me to slumber
twelve midnight is the hour of spooks
to render spirits for ancestral massaging
I refuse and keep shaking every time the jingle becomes
    irrelevant
blaring that irresistible tune "simunye … O' we are
    one …"
bang! kick the bloody box off
"simunye" … sè foot!

This is the country that knows how to impose
and cares less when it so does
'long as it is to make history.

I wondered why justice never pitched up these nights
if indeed she knew it was going to be this way
hope she has not gone to the dogs
while the law is made by asses in animal farm!

                                  MAISHE MAPONYA

# THE POWER-POINT POET
*April 2003*

He's been to the cemetery's heroes' section
Many times over
Bidding farewell to comrades gone
He's the living witness
Of those who've passed
Through the turmoil
Of struggle and paid with their lives.

The power-point poet
Who no longer can toyi
Sing
And chant
or dub
To the ululations
Of yesterday's
Freedom cravings.

He's the one who led that chant
Down Soweto road
Down every township road
Leading multitudes of marchers
Burning with anger
To wrench something
For struggle's sake.

Can you recognise him today
That one dressed in a pink tie
Addressing conferences in 5-star hotels
Ushering listeners through his dreamland
Power-point presentation

And they cheer
And they pay tribute
For his assumed power
He shares a table with the bank manager
Like he was never in it
Struggle
And he's poor no more.

Did you know he can't write poems anymore
Only Power-point presentations
For tender-preneurs who sit in line
For the next chunk of side-kick award
He exudes power
The Power-point poet!

                     MAISHE MAPONYA

# CAPE TOWN

High up on Ou Kaapse Weg
the wind of change blows
I spy a provocative sight below,
a bitter sweet location:
opposite Pollsmoor lies Steenberg Estate
two cultures, lives and fates,
one of golf and green,
the other concrete and grey.
My eye wanders to the dusty east
of the flats, the mythologised beast,
where imagination grows as the detail fades,
lives invisible in the distant haze.

Hugging mountains regal, crowned with cloud
and blue skies unblemished by doubt,
the suburbs, oozing purse power and grapes that rarely
    turn sour,
barely feel howls of a gail above
barely know Khayelitsha's love,
detached from the festering rage.
Despite the threat of change
the larnies look anything but paleas much as they might
    shout and rail
too snug, too close to the past to feel cold
too convinced by their story to be told.

Steenberg so close to the barbed life
suburbs so far from the flats' strife
yet *Polls* apart, *moor* different than a common country:
glamour mixed with grime,

pleasure with poverty not aligned
rands with ruin as neighbours:
golfers doing the inmates no favours
labouring the fairways as they labour the years the years
 observing snail change,
as platitudes try to hide the fears.

Indominatable, opaque and alluring,
Table Mountain continues to host the tourists –
holds firm against the times and weather
holds out against the future being better,
idealism now a wind-thinned leather.
A table on which the privileged feast
the tablecloth stained with old wine and cheese,
clouds of progress blown down the mountain
voices lost in the wind,
hopes pinned on 20 years and counting.
lying behind the grey walls
when the barbiturate haze falls
nothing is felt but buttons and boredom
no green or well trimmed freedom
but the 28's regal, crowned with lost years '94 onwards
 political spin-smeared.

High up on Ou Kaapse Weg
trees are visibly leaning over.
but out on the flats
lives are invisibly leaning over.
Steenberg trees stand tall, erect
Golfers swing clean, undaunted.

Across the roadin another world slowed
people are pecked
by choices and history haunted.

### CHARLES MARRIOTT

# JOHANNES SI BHEKE

Umuhle, unothile, uyakhazimula,
Amaphupho ayafezeka ku wena
Awu bhuke inkanyezi zo mbane
Weeh Ma, kuhle la
Kuth'wa la ku ka nyama ayipheli
Kuphela amazinyo endoda
Ngayeka umfino, ngakwhela isitimela
Nga fika kuwena
Nga fica izitrata zokuncola ne ndawo
Ezingena skhala sam
Awushongo yini, ukuthi la, inyama kudliwa eye ndoda
Kusale amazinyo wa khe encancazela estrateni
Eshumayela indlala
Igolide kade la thathwa
Johannes: si bheke
Ushiye abantu abangana amathuba, wa ba cindezela
Wa ba cikela phansi, se be gcine ba ne mkhuba
Bevulana ifuba ngo mese, be qgholozela inhliziyo
Kodwa uthando alubonakale
Inyembezi zam zinetha ngithi ngi cula
"Sinje nga majuba" kodwa unginqamule
Amaphiko, se ngiyingelosi engena mlondolozi
Johhanes ngi bheke ...
Umabonakude ungi bonisile ubucwebe
Ngabe e umabonaduze ngabe ngi funde ukuthanda
    okwam'
Johhaness ngiyeke

Ngi khathele okuphanda, nokusutha indlala
Johaness ngiyeke, ngikhumbule ekhaya
La umfuyo nga bantu,
Johannes ngiyeke, ngikhumbule impande.

                KELA MASWABI

# JOHANNES LOOK AT US

You are beautiful, you are rich, you shine
In you dreams do come true
Look at the stars as well
Lord, this is beautiful
They say this is where meat is in abundance
The only this that burns out are a man's teeth
I quit vegetables, I took the train
I arrived at your place
I found dirty streets all over
That violate my space
You didn't tell, that here, the only meat eaten is a man's flesh
What remains are his teeth scattered on the street
Preaching hunger
The gold was taken a long time ago
Johannes; look at us
You left people without opportunities, and oppressed them
You run them down, they ended up having attitude
Carving each other's chests with knives, gorging the heart
But we can't see love
My tears drip even as I sing
"we are like doves" but you nipped off
My wings, I'm now like an angel without a saviour
Johannes look at me
Television has shown me the jewellery
If it wasn't for television I would have learnt my own way of loving
Johannes leave me alone
I'm tired of hustling, of farting hunger

Johannes leave me alone, I miss home
Where wealth by people
Johannes leave me alone, I miss the homestead

*Translated from the isiZulu original – Kela Maswabi's*
*'Johanness si bheke' – by Goodenough Mashego*

# UPHAHLA

Uvuthuzile umoya obukade uxelwa
Zizanuse zezulu kumabonakude
Waxhalaba umakhulu
Lubhabhazil'uphahla
Afun'ukuphama amacangci

Uthe umama masobek'amatye

Sojongana kukuthembisela nokoyika
Lagqekreza lilenyez'izulu
Wakhalim'umakhulu esithi asinakuqabela ebusuku

Saseka ngelithi ngcono siwaphose phezu kwendlu

Iphokokile yona ixelisa unogumbe
Kwachichiza yonk'indawo ngesiquphe
Saqukeza sibek'izitya namabhakathi kuyo yonk'indawo
Sakhama amanzi, satshayela amanzi, sachitha amanzi
Wath'umakhulu uzakud'afe engekayifumani na eyakhe
    iRDP

Sajongana
Satsho ngazwi-nye yanga siyabhodla
*"Eyiphi makhulu, iyiyo nje lena?"*

Waqhwab'izandla umakhulu
Esithi bekungcono kwasetyotyombeni

       ZONGEZILE THEOPHILUS MATSHOBA

# THE ROOF

The winds that were forecasted
By the television climatologists have blown,
Much to Grandmother's agitation
The roof was shaken
Until its corrugated iron sheets threatened to loosen.

Mother instructed that we go put up some rocks
And we stared at each, frightened.
The thunderous sky afire with lightning,
Grandmother admonished us sternly,
That we date not climb on the rooftop at night.
We concluded to throw the stones up there instead.

The rain poured as though it were a storm
Bringing sudden showers all around.
We hurriedly placed dishes and buckets everywhere;
we dried the water, swept the water and threw out the water.
Grandmother asked if she'd die before she received her RDP house.

We looked at each other
And said in a chorus, as though burping;
"Which house, Grandmother, aside for this one?"
She clapped her hands, our Grandmother,
Saying it was better living in a shack.

*Translated from the isiXhosa original – Zongezile Theophilus Matshoba's 'Uphahla' – by Vuyokazi Ngemntu*

## GO DIKGAITŠEDI TŠA LEFSIFSI

Bo le ragetše ka thoko bophelo
Mahlong s baikaketši le ditshweša-mare
Le ge go le bjale le gatela pele
Gobane dikhukhuni le mekotla ya mašeleng
Ke mahlatse le mahlogonolo `phelong bja lena

Seo se le bileditšego mebileng ke khupamarama
Dilo tše bonagalago ke diabolose
Le iphile lešoka la nyaka borutho mebileng
Ka ge magae a fetogile
Felo la dintwa

Le fetogile masegafela
'Pelo tšona di rotha madi le meokgo
Ge le nagana bopelompe bja diroto-tša- mašialegare
Le gata tala e bola
Le atla bona babolai ba lena
La ba otla ka tladimolongwana
Mošomo o tšhaba diatla

KATISE MAWELA

# TO THE LADIES OF THE NIGHT

Life played you a bad hand
In the eyes of hypocrites you are disgusting
Regardless you keep walking
Because night trawlers and bags of money
Are blessings in your life

What sent you to the streets remains a mystery
What is seen is the Devil
You left home and seeked comfort on the streets
Since homes have become
Places of conflict

You are always laughing
Your hearts drip blood and tears
When you think the bad hearts of monsters
You keep walking
You hug even your very killers
You give them a kiss
Life goes on

*Translated from the Sepedi original – Katise Mawela's*
*'Go dikgaitšedi tša lefsifsi' – by Goodenough Mashego*

# IKASI LAMI

We township people, who call the township Kasi Lami
    with pride.
don't pride ourselves of the township's inception
We pride ourselves of the humans that exist in it
as they stand
firm as the rains flood their homes
houses
shacks on sandy dunes
that are not on firm ground.

We celebrate our children's creative ability
as their form games called
U three thini
Amagende
Umagalobha
in townships that lack playground spaces.

Its young gliding with smoothness
as they tap the streets with isipantsula
shacking off oppression.

We celebrate us
our humanity.

                          ONGEZWA MBELE

# PUINHOOP

'n Verbrande bedelaar.

Buite die hek stop hy my
met uitgedopte litchi-oë.
Karoobossies beur deur 'n geskroeide kop,
uitgebrande as binne 'n vleesdop.

Sy neus boei my:
'n herkonstuksie van 'n paraffiennag,
die dun papierlagie styf gespan,
die brandpad loop duskant die wang.

'n Bedelaar het verbrand.

                        MARTHÉ MCLOUD

# RUINS

A burnt beggar.

Outside the gate he stops me
with shelled litchi-eyes.
Karoo-bushes strain through a charred head,
burnt out ash in a fleshy sheath.

His nose intrigues me:
a reconstruction of a paraffin-night,
the thin paper-layer taut,
the fire-break lies this side of the cheek.

A beggar burnt to death.

*Translated from the Afrikaans original – Marthé Mcloud's*
*'Puinhoop' – by Pieter Odendaal*

# HO THABA BA ILENG

Ba tseba ba siile tatso e hlabosang Mzansi,
Mabitla ha a ratehe empa a bona a rateha a le jwalo,
Kgafetsa ba bososela hobane ba tutubetse,
Mahlo ha a ka buleha ba ka itshwara dihlooho tse masapo
    ka matsoho a masapo,
Ho raoha mobung o batang ha ke sa bua …

Sol Platjie o tsamaile a thabile, tshebetso a siile e ntle
Ha a tsebe ho setseng habo, Mzansi,
Ha a tsebe ho thulwana ka dihlooho ka palementeng,
A ka latola hore mona e ne e le habo.

John Dube ha a tsebe hore ANC e ntse e tsang,
A ka hlohlora dikatse tse nonneng mafura,
Tsa tseba hore o ne a e thehela eng,
E seng mejo e meharo, tjhelete,
Mophako wa manyekathipa o ka bonahala, wa eketseha ho
    fepa setjhaba.

Enoch Sotonga a ka fetola dintho
Nkosi Sikelel' iAfrika e ka fetoha
Ka lebaka le le leng,
Mosebetsi wa yona ha o sa bonahala,
Ho hlekehlekane ho feta serobeng sa nonyana,
Modimo wa Afrika, wa Afrika Borwa o kae?

Pososelo ya ntate Rolihlahla e ka makatsa ba bangata
E ka nyamele pele leihlo le panya,
O thabile hobane a ile a tseba Mzansi wa hae,

Naha e jele boya kajeno, batho ba fallela dinaheng tse ding.
 BoAustralia ba a tseba.
Mzansi ha esale ngwana-setsoha-le-pelo-ya-maobane.

Bohloko ba Mzansi bo omisa moko hara masapo a tiileng,
Bo tjhwatjhwatsa ho feta lekgopo le tlasa mahe a mabedi,
Ho feta lekgopo le pela mokoti o hlomphehang,
Bo fedise takatso ya bophelong ho ba phelang,
Ho thaba ba ileng hobane ha ba bone
Le ha ba utlwa, ke a hana, ha ba bone.

Nnete ya Mzansi e bipetsane,
E teteetsane ho feta moya o tswang nameng,
E teteeditse ba e tsebang, e tseka ho phatloha
Ba ileng e ba hlorisitse, ya tsekolla methapo ya bona,
Ba thabileng hobane ba phomotse,
Re sallane le tsona.

Nnete ya Mzazi e hana ka yona, e tswapetse
E tswapetse sa penti mafikeng a maholo, e hana ho
 tswapolleha,
E sitisa monga yona ho tsamaya, e kginne Afrika Borwa e
 tsejwang e le ntle,
Ho e tswapolla ke ho fahla batshwasi ba dithendara ka
 lehlabathe,

Afrika Borwa ya bapala thellisane boleleng,
Madi a ba ileng, a balwaneli ba tokoloho a fetoha thellisane
Ya thellisa hodima madi a bana ba batho,

Madi a qhitsitse ka sehlooho, le kajeno a ntse a llelwa ke
   beng ba bafu,
O potela ka mane ho bapalwa ka tokoloho, le ka mona ho
   jwalo.

Bofifi bo aperweng ke beng ba bafu ha bo bonwe,
Bo kwahetswe ke bobodu, manyofonyofo,
Lehlaba la lephako ke seitshireletso
Ba hana ba pipitletswe, ba ntse ba re ba lapile.
Ba ileng ba a thaba hobane ha ba bone tsena.

Maqeba a dikgutsana tsa bao ba ileng a ntse a bulehile,
A qhitsa ho feta sediba se kollang,
Ba llela ka dipelong bana ba batho, tse madi dikgapha tsa
   bona ha di tsebe kgefutso,
Ba lebohuwa ka masepa a metsi,
BoSlovo ha ba bone, ba a thaba tlasa mabitla a bona.

Thaka tsa ba ileng di ponne, esale di tshepiswa hona le
   hwane,
Ba se ba le makgatheng a lefu ho se nko ho tswa lemina,
Ba ntse ba kgotsa, "Lena lefatshe re a le tshaba, ho thaba
   ba ileng."
Le bona ba se ba tla ikela, ba se ba tla thaba le ba ileng
   phomolong e kgutsitseng ya bona.

BoOliver Tambo ha ba tsebe ba siile eng,
Diqaka di qakile ho feta diqaka tsa seqhaqhabola,
Mzansi wa batho o habodiswa seqhaqhabola se diqaka,
Hobane bophelo ke ho phela, re a phela

Mzansi ha re sa thabile rona, ho thaba ba ileng feela,
Thabo ya motsotswana ke eng?
Takatso e se e le yona ho ba latela,
Re tsebe ho thaba, re tla thaba ha re se re sa bone tse tlukutlang tsa lena lefatshe.
Mehwanto o ka tloha wa tsoha ho phatlalla le nahana hona jwale,
Matswantle a rotha madi, thepa yohle ya tjheswa jwalo ka mashala le patsi.

Ke itseng? Bona koranta e re bontsha tsona tseo,
Thelevishineng bona hle! Mamela seyalemoya se a paka le sona,
Facebook le Twitter ha ke sa bua, masetlapelo a bonahala le tjhabang le le dikelang,
Ba ileng ba a thaba, ke nnete.

THABISO MOFOKENG

# HAPPY ARE THOSE GONE

They know they left a sweet taste that salivates Mzansi
Graves are not loved but theirs get all the love
They smile because they are satisfied
If their eyes could open they would hold their skeletal
    skulls with bony hands
Not to mention jumping from the cold-cold soil

Sol Plaatjie left happy survived by his good work
he knows not what left at home, in Mzansi
he knows nothing about the confrontations in parliament
he would protest that this was his home

John Dube knows not what the ANC is up to
he would dust off fat cats
so they know what he fought for
not the feast of hawks, money
the food basket of the nation would nourish everyone

Enoch Sontonga would change things
Nkosi sikelel' iAfrica would change
At once
Its purpose is no longer seen
There's confusion beyond a bird's nest
Where is the God of Africa, South Africa?

Rolihlahla's candour would surprise many
It would disappear in no time
He is happy because he knew his South Africa
The country is today wasted, people are migrating to
    other countries. In Australia they know

South Africa is no longer the darling of the world

The pain of South Africa freezes marrow in strong bones
It ends the interest of life to those living
Happy are those gone for they cannot see
They can hear, but I protest that they can see

The truth of South Africa is congested
It's stiff than the soul leaving the body
It stiffens those who know, it promises to break
It bothered those gone, and tore off their veins
Those who are happy for they are rested
We are left behind to face everything

South Africa's truth it deniable, it's hidden
It's wedged like underwear in big bums, refusing to retract
It denies its wearer movement, it's restraining
South Africa known for its beauty
To unwedge it is to deny tenderpreneurs of opportunity

South Africa is skating on river fungi
The blood of those gone, freedom fighters become river fungi
It skates on the blood of others
Blood shed through brutality, that today still evoke cries from survivors
You look that way they play with freedom, even here is the same thing

The darkness covering families of the dead is unseen

It's hidden by laziness, shenanigans
Even when their stomachs are full, and they say they are hungry
The departed are glad they don't see this

The scars of the departed orphans are still open
They bleed than quick sand
They cry inside poor children, their mind know no rest
They are thanked with a bucket full of shit
Slovo and others don't see, they are glad in their graves

Peers of those gone are dry, since they were promised this and that
They are dying without having seen the promise
They declare, 'we are afraid of this world, glad are the departed'
They too will be gone, they will be in harmony with those long departed

Oliver Tambo doesn't know what he left
Heroes are heroic than heroes of ill-repute
Our South Africa is taught the deception of heroes
Since life is to for living, we are living
In South Africa we are not happy, happy are only the departed
What is happiness for a few seconds?

Our wish is to follow them

So we can be happy, we shall be happy when we no longer
 see the world's troubles
Marches can cease and wake up spread across the entire
 nation
Migrants are bleeding, their property burnt like trash

What did I say? Look at the newspaper and see the same
Look at the television! Listen to radio as it testifies to the
 same
Not mentioning Facebook and Twitter, tragedies are there
 when it rises and when it sets
The departed are indeed the happiest

*Translated from the Sesotho original – Thabiso Mofokeng's
 'Ho Thaba ba Ileng' – by Goodenough Mashego*

# DIFAQANE

We have a mulberry tree in our garden (it is not ours).
It grows on the other side of a white wall. Yawning

its branches over the electric fence that separates us
from our neighbours, it sheds its black fruit onto the
    grass.

The morning I came out to my mother,
all my lovers came out instead.

I saw my mother's horror rise as she watched them
claw themselves from my mouth, hands gripping

at my cheeks and jaw to squeeze themselves
into the air – one by one standing at my side

with gemmed eyes,
and bound breasts and lips like plums.

I saw my mother's horror rise, her eyes like salt-clouds
scanning the row, searching for Jehovah fruitlessly.

That same morning, I stepped into the garden with bare
    feet
plucked the berries from the ground, crawled

and ate the sun-warmed fruit
until my lips became black smudges.

Finally falling still,
sensing violence in the scattering.

    MANEO REFILOE MOHALE

# GAUTA O JA BATHO

Re kgobokanela Gauteng re tlilo sebetsa
Empa Gauta e a re thetsa
E sebetsana le rona, ha e sebelletse
Yona e a re sebedisa
Ha re sebedisane, ha re tshwarisane
Hang feela ra utlwa monate wa yona
Re fetoha baphaphathehi, hae re hana ho kgutlela
Rere hae menyetla e ya sokoleha
Ha re ka dula teng re tla sotleha
Re kampane ra dula Gauteng ra phophoreha
Ra iphelela seGauteng ra nahana se tla re thusa
Ka nnete hase re tsebe hase no re phutha
Ha re sa kgutlele morao re ilo ithuta
Re tla lla sa mmokotsane re sa shapuwa
Re lebale Sesotho rere ha re a se rutwa
Rere re kile ra e ba Basotho
Ha re ithuteng Sesotho ke sona se tla re thusa
Ka nnete se tla re phutha
Tsie e fofa ka mokota
Nonyana ha e fofe e sena ditshiba
Rona re tla phela jwang re sena setso
Ha re tlohelleng ho baleha sa mmutla
Re nahana hore re a ithusa
Kganthe re a itheola
Ke nako ya ho itjheola
Re tlohelle ho leba hae feela hare kula
O re ke hobaneng ba fatshe ba hana ho nesa pula
Menyako ba hana ho e bula
Rere hae mesebetsi e fedile ha re no dula
Re kampane ra dula Gauteng ya re duba

Ha o lebetse hae, Gauta e tla ho bolaisa thupa
Ka nnete e tla ho duba
Ha hona motho ya tla ho thusa
Ha o ka kgutlela hae batla ho thusa
Ba tla ho rarollela mathata
Gauteng ho thata
Batho re shebile a rona mathata
Re shebile tsa rona dithoto
Ba bohlale lefa la bona ke dithoto
Bula mahlo o shebe
O seke wa iphumana ole sethoto
O sebediswa ke babohlale
Hopola hore o mohale
Gauteng kaofela re batla ho busa
Empa ha re marena ha re tsebe ho busa
Gauta hae kgathetse ke rona e ya re tshwela
Thupa e sesane eya e tshela
Gauta ha e re jele batho ba ya re tsheha
Bare lefu leholo ke ditsheho
Empa hae ke botshabelo,
Gauta hle, re lokolle re kgutlele hae
O tlohelle ho re ja

## TSIETSI MOKHELE

# GOLD CONSUMES HUMANS

We gather in Joburg to work
But gold trips us
It deals with us, it doesn't work for us
It uses us
We don't work together, we don't assist one another
We don't get to taste its sweetness
We turn into the comforted, when it refuses to return
We say there are no opportunities at home
We rather stay in Joburg and fade away
Live the Joburg life and think it will help us
Indeed it knows not us it won't comfort us
We don't go back to learn
We'll cry hard without having been whipped
Forgetting Sesotho saying we were never taught
Say we we once Basotho
Let us learn Sesotho it will help us
Indeed it will comfort us
an army marches on its stomach
A bird can't fly without feathers
How will we live without culture
Let us stop fleeing like hares
Thinking we are helping ourselves
While we degrade ourselves
It's time to uplift ourselves
Stop going home only when ill
Have you wondered why our ancestors don't bring us rain
Refusing to open doors
We say there is no work at home we won't stay
We rather stay in Joburg and let it grind us
If you forgot home gold will whip you

Indeed it will grind you
No one will help you
If you return home they will help you
They will solve your problems Joburg is tough
We are looking at our own problems
We looking at our own properties
The clever one's wealth is properties
Open your eyes and see
Don't turn into a fool
Being used by clever people
Remember you are a fighter
In Joburg we all want to rule
But we don't have chiefs we don't know how to rule
When gold is tired of us it spits on us
It whips us with a thin whip
When gold has consumed us people laugh
They say the hardest death is being laughed at
But home is refugee
Gold please free us let us return home; don't consume us

*Translated from the Sesotho original – Tsietsi Mokhele's
'Gauta o ja batho' – by Goodenough Mashego*

# YET MORE STONES

Nelson Mandela has died twice:
once in Rivonia, out of the sun,
on a Monday, and once in Johannesburg,
on a Friday in December, which was not
without its own sun – if not bright spot.

The first time he died, he was thinking
of Jesus Christ, who died in Jerusalem,
maybe on a Thursday, surely in darkness?
Jesus died again, not of an unknown illness
but of love – as fictionalised by Matthew?

And Brothers, said Biko, his last Wednesday
in Pretoria, you must die once in Soweto,
in the land of gold and before going you
must write to them or bring in trash bins
filled with dreams.

So Brothers, I will die, maybe on a Sunday,
out of the way, because today it is Sunday,
and their words are jamming the road to
freedom and there is nowhere to put these
words that keep recalling all those other
words, like stones on more stones ...

on more stones
on more stones.

GEORGE MOMOGOS

# VERGANGENHEITSBEWAELTIGUNG[1]

his little girl sweet in the picture
in the pretty dress his mother made
I pray no one does to his daughter
what he did to me
I promise I suffer no schadenfreude[2]

### JACKIE MONDI

---

[1] vergangenheitsbewaeltigung – German: coping with the past
[2] schadenfreude – German: pleasure felt at the misfortune of others

# A HUNGRY STOMACH HAS NO EARS

Charred bodies hanging off power lines,
Making news headlines.
Izinyoka[1] have struck once more
The electricity struck back this time
Tomorrow another one will try
A hungry stomach has no ears

Decomposing corpses trapped in mines
Searching for the golden windfall
Zama-zamas[2] on a quest
A rock fall sealed their fortune
Another will take a dig at the hidden treasure
A hungry stomach has no ears

Pubescent nipples pierce her paltry top
Filling in for her mother who is sick
Truck drivers lick their tongues
She takes a loaf of bread home
And the affliction that grounded her mother
A hungry stomach has no ears

But, a greedy stomach has no conscience.

JACKIE MONDI

---

[1] Izinyoka – electricity thieves
[2] Zama-zamas – illegal miners

# VARIATIONS IN COLOUR

*red*
Your eyelids lift like shutters and pass a torch across her body. The scent of your beer-stained breath makes her legs twist into a pretzel. You both already understand how she will fold into the crook of your arm and tug at her nightshirt as it rolls up to her breasts. The world you inhabit is a deep basin – wet and warm – and you both peer into it, seeing yourselves in your lives before.
*orange*
She is in love with you. Her stomach knots in this realisation and she leaves the room as queasiness sets in. It is an abomination of feeling: her affections turn against her. She now lives in captivity: no day is complete without you. She weeps at the thought of never inhabiting only her own experiences again.
*yellow*
She examines the world like a fat lemon in her palm. Its surface is uneven, pocked and scarred; the face of a jaundiced, pimply teenager. She draws a map with a Swiss knife on it, showing you the segments of fruit that were once her juicy, plump motherland. But – she demonstrates with her Swiss knife – segments have been chopped out. She hands the slice to you, urging you to devour it. You suck it timidly – sicken – and then toss it into the bin.
*green*
She spots the withering bloom on your windowsill, a gift that she had given you – dying. *What does it take to let a succulent die?* she ponders. Her mouth is dry with despair.
*blue*
She arches her foot out like a feline, sending it on a mission

from under the duvet to test the air. She is not ready for the world to be much the same as it was yesterday and she quickly retreats, curling like a snake inside a muddy nest.
*indigo*
The bird dives into her lap. She is confused, *this is not what birds do*. It flaps – madly, crossly – a tantrum. She smiles and spreads her legs generously to free it from the clutches of cloth. But when it unfurls, the bird stares her down and tilts its head in inquiry. But she does not yet know how to talk to birds.
*violet*
Light cuts open the greying womb, a surgical precision that reveals the bald head of the Sun, protruding forward, as it spills out into the world. Nursed by the dew on soft, sleepy branches, it takes tentative steps across the tops of trees. Then, bursts forward into the full expanse of sky. Reckless, uncertain vibrancy. The shimmer of the youthful day grazes her shoulder, but she has lived too long to be enthused by such showy repetition. She waits patiently for dusk and then smiles.

NEDINE MOONSAMY

# LANIWANI

Huddled into a police van few hours before, for skinning
*nkwahle* – the land iguana that loves rocks. The land
iguana, a delicate meal he relished. But the green
police called it murder, or inciting extinction.

And so Laniwani asked, bending backwards as if staring at
the courtroom roof: where was the *nkwahle* family - the
complainants in the case - the mother or the uncle or
the aunt at least.

When no one could point at a *nkwahle* in the courtroom,
and someone said "the State" but could not point at
anything; Laniwani stepped down demanding to be
unchained. The *nkwahle* family had no quarrel with his
meal. And the magistrate smiled, ordered him
uncuffed.

MOSES MTILENI

# THE HOUSE WE BUILT

'We are building Africa'
They said
Tears down their faces
Fists clenched in passing courage
Voices hoarse, seared by betrayal
Torsos curved, by starvation

      o

How like younglings, them we believed
And behind them, our weight threw
Giving them all, that we had
Sending our kids to sleep, on single straws
With bellies growling, hunger on them feasting
'Hungry, we are hungry,' children wept
'They are building a new world,' solemnly to them we said
If only wisdom had struck then

      o

'We are building Africa'
They said
As we, like slaves, in blood and hunger
That house built
Whilst they stood, baton and pistol in hand
Keeping order and law, as they said
Shooing us back and forth, like plaque infested beings
'Build!, build!' they shouted
And in haste and fear, that house built
'We are building Africa', they said

      o

Swiftly then, did our kindness flee
And vices in us, there found a home

And never again, did our faces shine
On altars holy and in high places
Nor our knees, again to the ground went
To praise and pray, the divine above
Not even from our lips, did those hymns flow
As poverty and hunger, in might came
And like a wild fire, decimating all on its path
'Building Africa', they said
And like children, them we believed

○

Unbearable then, life became
As against each other, we fought
And sent to Hades, both stranger and friend
As more cruel, surviving became
And father, down strong wine went
Drowning themselves, as apart they fell
And young lads, their sisters raped
That spirited will, going to waste
As mothers too, into harlotry they daughters sent
And others, lifting their skirts to live
As poverty attacked all, both young and old
'We are building Africa'
Behind closed doors, they shouted still

○

In multitudes then, did we die
A feast for dogs and birds of the sky
And darker, the world became
That brilliant flame, that once shone
Now blown away, by huge winds

Which brought countless, ills and pains
To nail the last screw, on what was
A paradise, where only virtue was known

○

Very late then, did wisdom come
And like a flame, up we rose
To fight for the little, that was left
Of the great past, that in ignorance lost
But weak and inspirited, our revolution was
And quickly, down it went
For there can be no loyalty, in an empty belly
Not even patience, on the face of instant wealth

○

'We are building Africa'
They said
Bellies bulging, proud promontories
Pockets bursting, full of gold and coin
Their stuffed bodies, buried deep
On cotton soft, cushions
And voices hoarse, from ceaseless shouting
'We are building Africa', they said
In luxury draped, in comfort surrounded
'We are building Africa,' they said
As inside that house, they sat
The one we built, in pain and hunger.

SIFISO MTSHALI

## "TO MOS DEF IN THE WOOLWORTHS QUEUE"

yo Yasiin Bey, welcome to the neighbour
hood. I have always wondered who buys those
plastic-fibre 'Imagine NO RhiNOs'
carry-alls they sell at the tills for a
pink Randela each. turns out it's 40-
something ex-pat visa-less Brooklynite
rappers starting a new life for themselves
in the most unequal city in the
NEXT CUSTOMER TELLER 5 PLEASE HAVE
   YOUR
WOOLWORTHS AND MYSCHOOL CARDS READY
   fuck man,

have you just bought like two grands' worth of fruit
and raw cashews? even by my standards
that's a bit opulent *no thanks I don't
need a bag* you're chatting with all the till
ladies and they all seem pretty chuffed with
*no, no cards ma'am* I don't think they can quite
understand that Black Star drawl, but still. yeah,
maybe it's just that aura that famous
people have. you know, Yasiin – or Mos, hey,

Mr Def – this reminds me of the time
I thought I saw Annie Lennox in the
Pick n Pay in Camps Bay, when I saw her
buying Häagen-Dazs, right off of buying
up more property in the area,
driving up my already-sizable

rent. all I want to do is live in the
City Bowl, Mr Def, that's all I want.
*ja cheque please* Mr Def, why are you here

at the Kloof Street Woolworths. all I want is
my sugar-free ginger beer and single
Granny Smith and here you are reminding
me about how I will never make it
onto the property ladder. I want
to take a picture of this for Rachel.
she told me once she was at a party
with Teju Cole and someone thought he was
you, Mr Def, Mr Bey, and this

chick kept on buying Teju Cole drinks all
*yeah no, I'm good thanks. brought some bags today*
*ha-ha yeah, gotta save those fifty cents*
*when you can.* I suppose, Mr Def, if
I were to ask you a question *yeah sure*
*thanks have a lovely day too ma'am* it would
be, "Mr Def, Mr Bey, do people
mistake you for Teju Cole while you're out
here, oscillating in and out of court

and my local Woolworths with Kanye West
on speeddial?" Mr Def, Mr Bey, hey,
let me take a picture as I walk past
you with my phone aloft, hey let me –
you turn. you look me in the eye, and I
put my phone back into my pocket. we

walk out the Woolworths together, onto
Kloof Street, and I go home to write this poem
instead.

                      NICK MULGREW

# FOUR MINUTES

A few minutes ago, the car broke down
                         again, stationed outside the park,
on the middle of the road,
             like a boat navigating through a desert.
The cars behind us start hooting.
             I want to keep them quiet like flutes,
but come to think of it, I shouldn't panic.
                 I have witnessed this before:
at seven, when he was discharged,
             we lost our way between entrances
                       and
exits and everything in between,
             before moving out of the hospital.
We drove on a road that would lead us
             home, and then the car broke down,
                   so it had
to be pushed, devoid of any
             muscle, I had to run to ask for help.
When I returned, he had left,
             four minutes, that's all it took,
                   and he
was still in a stationary car.
             The cars behind us slowly move past us.

                           LUTHANDO NCAYIYANA

# THE BARKSOLE MAN

We look up startled from our books.
"It's just the kudu," I say.
*Just* the kudu?
They've come to lick the salt.
Drink water from the bird bath.
The male's curved horns glint
as he dips under the branches.

And I think of the Barksole man.
He tells me he loves the bush too
when I take in old boots for new soles.
"Jis, I miss it," he says "Kudus are my
favourite buck."
I nod enthusiastically.
"There's nothing like it, hey, when you
lift your rifle ..."

That's when the Barksole man and I
part ways.

## PAMELA NEWHAM

# TO THOSE FLUTTERING BEINGS

Fire, blue-flamed fire burns in the youth!

From the orchard of poverty
Fresh from nests perched on a million withered trees
  a bird learns that it too can sing, can fly and
    understand anew the liberating freedom of wafting airs

Its wings flap violently
Its voice a bellow of an unknown measure of its own
    breath-span
Its beak pokes and burrows into all typed sores
Its claws riddle the land with asymmetric anger of self
    discovery

Through all this chaos
This young bird has found its voice
This ripe bird has shed its ignorance
This lithe bird flutters in utter revolt
This awoke bird has left its mothers nest,
    and now sings long and deep into the blue night

shattering the sturdiness of trees as they fall
    wings flapping to the rhythm of fees must fall.
And now
I too have learned why the caged bird sings!

It is for the sweet idyll that revolution springs

Freedom!

                      MANDLA ROBERT NGAKANE

# NOT ANOTHER NURSE'S TALE

How hard it must be for those who tender to horror daily
Spreading some young thing's legs apart
poking and dabbing with prudent care
What magic healing poetry or sharp fangs
their words are at that moment of vulnerability

Of what sorrow tales – that drape their tongues – do they carry to their homes

Miners talk of unrefined gold and rough diamond discoveries
Farmers tell of the magic amour between nature.
a romance of seed, soil, sun and waters

But of what harrowing ordeals fill and dry mouths of care givers
What tales do they tell to their beloved
Is it not of ruptured hymens and bloodied thighs
Of hope snatched with evil clutch
Is it not of children pilfered of the curios gleam in their moon-like eyes

Innocence despoiled through their legs
Blood gushing from torn flesh & prospects of motherhood ending while disease and virus spreads.

How hard it must be for those mothers who carry those horrors home to their daughters. To their husbands. To their sons.

But how harder it must be for them to whom those
 horrors have become their reality and not just another
 nurses tale.

        MANDLA ROBERT NGAKANE

# A THANKLESS LABOUR

Mothers of black boys, beware:
You whose brood has ebony skin and kinky hair;
do not let him venture too far, even as he gets older.
Beauty, they say, is only in the eye of the beholder
and the beast
will insist
that your child appeared armed
Though he will be the one bleeding, dead or harmed
If you're lucky, you'll see him dragged away in chains
while some less fortunate mother cries for her boy's
    remains!
These graves have an insatiable appetite for boys with
    God in their DNA
and the media
is even greedier
to put their maimed,
unnamed
bodies on display.
Descendants of forgotten dynasties,
these heirs of erased deities
reared on battle cries disguised as lullabies;
our sons learnt to run before they could crawl.
Bred to win every game of football
so they can kick poverty to the curb
and buy their siblings a home in some white suburb,
drowning in debt that's thicker than water.
Some are driven to death
Chasing heaven on earth
across the border.
Why, my womb mourns these suns every full moon -

Lord knows I bore my first fourteen years ago at eighteen,
 on the 18th of June
and yet two more
whom my heart follows out the door;
paving their paths with hushed prayers.
This inimba has too many layers:
We want out sons fierce, brave and bold
yet we demand them back from the world
lest they not find their way home in one piece.
We ghetto mothers are strangers to peace!

                        VUYOKAZI NGEMNTU

# THEY NEVER DIED

They are still alive, Mama
They breathe, and eat and bleed
They hope and dream and feel
They raise children
They are loved
They cry
They give in to changing tides
They are still alive

They question the sanctity of the gods
They dare the devil
They dance with our daughters of night
They pray.
They believe.

My brother, your son, Mama
Stands guard at their gate
Protects their children
Lays his life for their animal
And kills my lovers for their sanity
He has died inside
But they are still alive

The men who took Tata out of jail,
Made a mockery of his manhood
Stripped him off his dignity
And fed him to the dogs
They are still alive

BOMIKAZI NJOLOZA

# ILIZWE LAM

Ndinga ndingahamba nanini na ndiye apho ndifuna ukuya khona
Ndinga ndingahamba naxesha nini ndibuke indalo ka Mdali
Ndinga ndingabalitsha – ntliziyo umxolelanisi umthambisi wentliziyo
Ndinga ndingashiya indlu yam ivuliwe kodwa umakhelwane ayivale engebanga nto

Ndinga ndingahamba esitatweni ndinyantsule ndingenavalo lokukhuthuzwa
Ndinga ndingaqhuba isithuthi sam ndivule iifestile ndingenavalo lokuxhonyiswa

Ndinga ndinganxiba isigqebezana sam ndibethwe lilanga ndihambe ngokukhululeka

Ilizwe lam uMzantsi Afrika utshaba lwam

Koda kube nini na ndizivaleleke ngaphakathi kwengcango zomzi wam
Koda kube nini na ndisentolongweni kumasang' omzi wam
Kwakuvakala izingqi ndixhuma ndicambalale phantsi okwenyoka
Ndingashukumi ndilindele ukushukunyiswa kwesango lokungena
Ibethele ukuma intliziyo lunge ucango luyatyhilizwa

Ilizwe lam uMzantsi Afrika utshaba lwam
Mikhulu imibhalo yamaphephandaba ecaleni kwendlela
Ichaza udaba lokudlwengulwa nokubulawa kwabasetyhini
   nabantwana
Lomgama abalikrele elintlantlu-mbini nelihlaba
   entliziyweni yam

Lindicanda kubini uphume umphefumlo wam ngenxa
   yentlungu
Ndisive isikhalo solosizi obelungenamlweli namhlanguli

Ndizibone ezonyembezi zixananaze umbombo zisiya
   ezantsi
Ilizwe lam uMzantsi Afrika utshaba lwam

Ndinga ndingosululela uluntu ngobubele imbeko
   nokukhathalela omnye
Ndinga ndingangena umzi nomzana

ndivakalise uxolo nicwangco
Ndinga ndingabamba umboko ndisasaze indaba
   ezilungileyo
Ndinga ndinga hamba ndichazele bonke onyana nentombi
   ze Afrika uthando lwam

Ndinga ndingahamba ndibange ngolwango lothando
   ndithi 'niyathandwa'
Ndinga ndingafumana ithuba ndibaqinisekise ukuba
   bazalelwe injongo

Ndinga ndingabajonga emehlweni ndithi kubo sekwanele
 izikhali phantsi

Ndinga ndingabaqinisekisa ukuba mabavuke
 ebuthongweni baphakame emaqandeni
Ndinga bangayazi inyaniso yothando, ndinga bangayazi
 ukuba bazalelwe injongo.

Bazalelwe injongo.

Uzalelwe injongo.

                              AMANDA NODADA

# MY COUNTRY

I wish I could leave anytime
And go wherever my wanderlust leads
I wish I could, at any time,
Return to God's creation.
I wish I were a hero,
A harbinger of peace, a comforter of hearts.
If I were to leave my house unlocked
And have my neighbour lock it without stealing its contents.
How I wish I could roam the streets freely,
Gallivanting with no fear of being robbed.
I long to drive my car with the windows rolled all the way down,
Not fearing the possibility of being highjacked.
That I should be at liberty to walk around in my miniskirt and feel the sun's rays caressing me.

In this country of mine, South Africa,
That has become my arch nemesis.

For how long will I have to continue
Locking myself indoors
And remain a prisoner behind the walls of my own home?
I jump up with fright at the slightest sound,
Prostrate myself on the floor like a snake,
And remain motionless
Dreading the sound of my front door unlocking
As my heart beats itself into a deadly stupor,
Convinced that the door is being pushed open.
Oh, my beloved South Africa,

Metamorphosed into my enemy!
Bold are the headlines on the roadside
Covering the subject of rape, femicide and infanticide
And such words become a multi-pronged spear
In piercing my heart
And splicing it into two
Until my soul exits my body
From the debilitating pain
As I hear the deafening cries of that poor thing
With neither a defender nor a redeemer
And I see those tears
Sprawled across such a face, falling down.
This country of mine, South Africa,
That has become my foe!

I wish I could contaminate society
With benevolence, respect and empathy.
If I could visit every homestead and every cottage at large,
And sound a call for peace and harmony.
I wish I could grab the mic and spread good news.
How I wish I could travel far and wide
To tell all the sons and daughters of Africa of the love
    inside me
If I could employ my supernatural powers
And let them know 'You are all loved!'
Oh, if I were afforded a chance
To assure them that they were born to fulfil a divine
    purpose .
I wish I could look deep into their eyes and announce,
    "Enough! Put down your weapons.'

How I wish I could implore them
To awaken from their slumber and rise
I wish they knew the truth about love
I wish they knew they were born to serve a divine purpose.
Indeed, born to serve a divine purpose they were!
You too were born to serve a divine purpose!

*Translated from the isiXhosa original – Amanda Nodada's 'Ilizwe Lam' – by Vuyokazi Ngemntu*

# CASSETTE

i could never bring myself
to ask my mother
the artist and title
of the cassette tape
that my uncle was killed for

in the streets of kwa-mashu
the murderer still walks
his footsteps block out
our moments of silence

                SIHLE NTULI

# "REFLECTION"

On the flat green lawn
at the Pretoria[1] Union Buildings[2]
I sit alongside grandpa
on a long stretched grey wooden bench
with his attention span
directed somewhere
his right index finger points
to his round crystal spectacles
lying on the long bridge of his nose
cautiously inspecting
the Sunday Times[3] newspaper
in his big veined hands
reading the headline:
"FEES MUST FALL"

Grandpa shakes his head
wimping a whisper
some unknown guilty conscience arises
for a moment, he is quiet
then admits by saying:
"We have failed the youth,"
I raise an eyebrow
"Yes, it is true," he continues
"Toyi-toying[4] was part of apartheid,[5]
now we have passed it on

to the young at heart
who vandalise school buildings
and burn tyre wheels
in order to be heard!"

          LAZOLA PAMBO

---

[1]  Pretoria is the capital city of South Africa
[2]  Union Buildings is a building of the official seat of South African government in Pretoria
[3]  Sunday Times is one of South Africa's larger weekend newspaper
[4]  Toyi-toying means a dance step performed at protest gatherings or marches
[5]  Apartheid means a policy or system of segregation or discrimination on grounds of race

# BLACK JOY

We were spanked for each other's sins
We were spanked in syllables and by the word of God
Before dark mean: home time
My grandmother's mattress knew each of my sibling's,
    and cousin's and neighbour's children's morning
    breath by name.
A single bedspread on the floor was enough for all of us.
Bread slices were buttered with irama and rolled into
    sausage shapes; we had it with black rooibos. We did
    not ask for cheese. We were filled
My cousins and I gathered around one bowl of
    umngqusho, each with his or her spoon.
Sugar water completed the meal. We are home & whole
But
Isn't it funny, that when they ask about black childhood,
    all they are interested in is our pain, as if the joy parts
    were accidental?
We write love poems too
But you only want to see our mouths torn open in protest,
    as if our mouths were a wound with pus and gangrene
    for joy.

                              KOLEKA PUTUMA

# RESURRECTION

The soil is bleeding trauma
The memory says let me out
The massacre says, remember me
The soil says, it still hurts
The skeletons point to where it does

The blood says, find me on the perpetrators hands
The blood says, wash me from the victims' body

The blood says, do not let the children see the bath
The blood says, do not let the youth wash in it

The blood says, the grave is no place for healing

There is enough blood to map the countries it has flooded
There is enough blood lost for us to die
There is enough blood left for us to live

There is enough blood to say their names
Enough blood to remember them by birth
Their tongues are burning in our mouths
When we talk about our history, we put the fire out.

                                        KOLEKA PUTUMA

# BEDTIME STORIES FOR OUR LITTLE GIRLS

He will break your heart.
He will cut you open
From your chest to your abdomen.
He will get life
You will get death.

Valentine's Day dinner
With your lover
Who will soon be your killer.
4 shots
But he loves you lots.
He will get 6 years
You will get 6 feet.

You are on honeymoon
With your beloved groom.
He loves you to death.
So much so
He may have organised a bullet to your neck.
He will walk free
Because the case lacks consistency.

Rest
In
Peace.

SIBONGILE RALANA

# A PENNY FOR YOUR THOUGHTS

No offence
But why do black people laugh
The way they do?
I'm not racist though.

No offence
But why do black people smell
The way they do?
I'm not racist though.

No offence
But why do black people look
The way they do?
I'm not racist though.

No offence
But why do black people talk
The way they do?
I'm not racist though.

No offence
But why do black people go to the beach
The way they do?
I'm not racist though.

No offence
But why do black people
Live ... be ... breathe ...
exist?

SIBONGILE RALANA

# POWER

He walks toward the car:
it's an ordinary autumn day in Johannesburg.
Stiffening, but the doors are locked, I check,
and the bag's in the boot.
He stares, I clench my hand around the steering wheel,
diminished in my seated position.
He looks at me: his eyes bore through.

He walks past, I stare at his departing back.
His shirt has holes in it, and his jeans are
shabby, hanging off his skinny frame.
His saunter diminshed:
I hold all the cards now, car, house, money for food.
Feeling foolish. I wait for the light to turn green,
I smile sheepishly at no one in particular.

ARJA SALAFRANCA

# COLLATERAL DAMAGE

She lies as though asleep
her teddy cuddled close
– the teddy is stained

Detonations quake the building, walls tremble, windows
    break
she smiles gently – she does not stir, nor wake.
The stain slowly spreads

Bomb-loosed dust sifts softly down,
settles silently on an unblemished cheek – she does not
    sneeze nor blink.
The stain is ruby red

Sirens shriek and women wail,
she, softly sunlit, is still
The stain is turning rusty

They break the door, frantically shift the rubble,
lift her gently, limply, asking – urgently – Muslim or Jew?
The teddy cannot answer –
he has bled to death,
and his blood stains us all.

                              FERDIE SCHALLER

# THE BURNING MAN

The crowd screams

He burns brightly, eyes – incandescent
fingers weeping flesh – imploring
lipless mouth pleads – silently
a policeman watches – unmoving
he crawls – chameleon slow

The crowd roars

rocks smash down – unfeeling
he does not crumple – crumble
grey ash-body trembles – disintegrating
a policeman fires an extinguisher – casually
his crater-mouth pleads

The crowd growls

he emerges from the retardant fog – slowly
flames creep across his back – flickering
not crawling, just shuddering – anguished
the policeman kicks a skinny dog – disinterested
a steel bar descends – mercilessly

the crowd hisses

he subsides – melting
road-kill – steaming
on the pitted tar – a shadow

the policeman walks – upwind
he convulses – lies still

The crowd sighs

The dog licks his face – lovingly
His eyes are open – staring
Does he see the rainbow
 in the already buzzing fat glistening green latrine flies?
The policeman tosses a discarded box over the discarded
    man

The crowd chatters as it leaves

                        FERDIE SCHALLER

# BOOTS FOR LITTLE BOYS

There are some little boys –
all elbows, ears and knobbly knees –
who love boots
not shiny Sunday church shoes, nor hard Monday school shoes
not sleek soccer boots, nor even rugged rugby boots
not soft slippers nor takkies nor trainers –
but dad's scuffed safety shoes and big boet's dusty army boots.

There are some little boys
with furious frowns – and lazy, longing smiles
who love big boots –
who know boots are for
miners and marines and mountaineers,
and brave drummer boys

There are some little boys
with magpie minds –
all wonder and wishes and magic and mystery –
who love strong boots –
for walking and marching and crunching
across mountains and fire and ice.

There are some little boys
down at heel, scraped and unpolished-
unlaced - with their tongues hanging out,
who love old boots –
boys who like to shout:
"Magnetogorsk and Manitoba & Mlabathini and

Mariepskop"
And hear the echo of other, older times.

There are some little boys
 who love big old strong scuffed boots –
because big boots are for big boys
who can't be bullied and beaten
and made to cry.

                        FERDIE SCHALLER

# OOGAF

kyk al die oë:

ster-iris son-dop aard-bal
die halfmaan-lid

en hier, kort-
stondig en intiem:

knie-kop kneukel-traan nawel-knip.

om gesien te word. ag,
my dawerende, my lapperende, my lewe.

maar dáár – in die boom – 'n knoets
bewaar in jare se jare: ou houtoog

dié sien.

                      KARIN SCHIMKE

# AT A GLANCE

behold all the eyes:

star-iris sun-shell earth-ball
the halfmoon-lid

and here, short-
lived and intimate:

knee-cap knuckle-tear navel-wink.

to be seen. oh,
my roaring, my patched, my life.

but there – in the tree – a bur
preserved in years' years: a wooden eye

which sees.

*Translated from the Afrikaans original – Karin Schimke's
'Oogaf' – by Pieter Odendaal*

# UNCLE TOM

Uncle Tom has been in the family as far as I can remember
Abo mcane ba biz'u baba a black sheep[1]
A license in need of renewal
An entrepreneur
Man that can sell the skin off his home along with his soul

Kantle ba re[2]
'we've got an uncle in the furniture business …
Ka sekhoa a whore!'[3]
Or sell out
Fela ke nnete[4]

The bones of my brothers and sisters seem to make for quite the profitable venture
While vulture skinned leather seats and freshly cut curtains
Coupled with a couple of carpet corpses make a sturdy foundation
For such a standard of living

At dinner
He seats himself where my father would be sitting
If he ever came home for supper
Or came home at all
Either way my mother still dishes for his absence to remind u'Tom
Kuthi she's married
Kotwa[5] he's patient with his pawns
Because he sees it in black and white

That he seizes our days as he becomes our knight
We forget how he makes his money because we sleep on it
I'm ashamed
Because nowadays even I can't sleep without it

And I'm afraid for my soul
For even I have started to wear designer issues
Like my uncle Tom
A man of means meant for bigger things and better people
Dressed in polished Epaulettes and drenched in posh palettes
A man well versed in the culinary art of fine dying

You can find him in high places getting higher off our poverty
My apologies
*Your* poverty

I've recently been promoted unfairly
And barely managing to catch scraps of conversation falling from the dinner table
I've been able to ascertain my position in this family
A pawn like my mother

Who hopes to be a queen one day
Moving step by step
Dancing around emotions family members fail to get off their chess
I'm board with kitchen politics but hold no seat at the bedroom

Where family fortunes unfortunate secrets spill before
 people go to sleep
Only my aunt screams at that table
The walls are thin
But we live in a glass house
So no one hears her getting stoned

They only see the bloody footprints in the mornings
But we walk on each other's broken flaws
To keep our skeletons close and our closets even closer
So everyone turns a blind blue eye to my uncle

My uncle Tom
A lover of fine whine
Whether it's his woman complaining or bleeding or crying
She white washes down his throat all the same

And the women in the house stay quiet
Their voices also boxed in his throat
They only speak when spoken to
Only when pregnant with his heirs can they breathe

Wondering
Where are their husbands?
Wandering
Outside their marriages
Outside their responsibilities
Outside their homes
We don't speak of these men in this house

My uncle is one of these men
In another house
Holding my tongue
My mother wants to keep him happy

Hobane a tseba tlala[6]
She knows I wouldn't eat without him
Right now she can only pray
That when I grow up I don't become him

But prayer doesn't put food on the table
He does

KORI SEFEANE
*Sesotho-English translation by
Goodenough Mashego*

---

[1] my aunts call father a black sheep
[2] out there they say
[3] in English a whore!
[4] it's the honest truth
[5] but
[6] because she knows hunger

# AUSCHWITS

Auschwits
Outfits
Housed in
Apartments out in
The cold parts meant for animals
And criminals

Gauteng
But no parchment
Brown skin has turned garment
Houses have lost families
Ubuntu
Ke mali

Imali
Ke batho
Motho
Ke oli o mots'o
Ha a sootho
Ke phoofolo[1]

Our spirit animal is the zebra
Our apparent apparel is half sponsored
Re apere Africa[2]
But we're wearing Afrique de Suid

We are freaks
In suits who
Still speak sotho with their mothers
Sewed into our skin and coats

We are sawed in two
Our kin and coating
Quoting

Not the words of our ancestors but our insurance policies
Hippo-
Crits we've
Put our bloodlines on hold

And now our calling is impotent to us
Becaues we form ties with individuals
And knot
Communities

Lately we've been turning cheeky with our mothers
In tongues we speak
Our mother tongue is tongue in cheek
We are quoting

Not the words of our ancestors
But our insurance policies
The history books will read: we lost our concentration,
    camping in the US

But they will be written out of context
In past tense by foreign mense making sense of our
    experience as usual

Our stories will be those
Not taught to our children in schools

Only covered partly in lectures passed through
 documentaries and books
Trying to accurately describe our lives

But books can only do so much with pictures
Pictures only draw so much colour
colour only spills so much blood
Only bones can navigate through time
And this time

The bones have themselves to pick with you

KORI SEFEANE
*Sesotho-English translation
by Goodenough Mashego*

---

[1] humanity; is blood; money; is humans; a human being; is black oil; he is not brown; it's an animal.

[2] we are wearing Africa

# FIX ME

They said they would fix me
I was completely unaware that I was broken to start with, but they seemed determined to dismantle me
To take me apart into tiny pieces and put me back together the way they saw fit

It was a night like any other
And I was walking home like I had always done
This street had memorised my footprints
I had used this route since I was six
It really was a night like any other or so it seemed
Until I spotted him
A shadow lurking between the rays of that dimly lit street light
The one that's never worked quite right
I immediately dropped my gaze, pulled my cap down, pushed my hands into my pockets, added a little bounce to my step and prayed,
"Dear God. Please make him blind to the slight swell of breasts under my shirt or the lack of bulge in the crotch of my pants. Make him believe that I am just some random dude walking down the street"
My prayers must have fallen on deaf ears
Because the only response I received were whistles and loud jeers from three other shadows fast approaching from behind me
It was then that I realised that this howling pack of wolves was on the hunt
And I was their intended prey
My heart attempted to escape my chest cavity

My brain spoke a language my legs could not decipher
I was frozen
"Beg for mercy," I thought
But the words barely made it past my larynx
When I felt a hand tightly grip my trachea
He pulled me into his embrace and whispered almost
    lovingly
"I will make you a real woman even if it kills you"
He said it was his God given right to violate me
His heavenly duty to exorcise this lesbian demon from me
To rape me into conformity
It's funny how saints and sinners are so perfectly aligned
    in darkness
They say man was created in God's likeness
But I looked upon the face of Lucifer that night
Eyes devoid of any soul's reflection
I tried to fight, but my limbs were pinned down
This was my crucifixion, but whose sins was I to die for?
The courage to exist in my own truth, to them, was worth
    spilling my blood for
I tried to scream, but my cries for help were muffled
    against the heaving chest of whoever's turn it was
A piece of my soul stolen with each planted seed
Demons hellbent to break my spirit
Or were they heaven sent?
I mean, if God really is all seeing and all powerful
Then why would He allow such atrocities
Except to satisfy His own saddistic tendencies
Go ahead, call it blasphemy!
Maybe they raped the faith out of me

The pain poured out of my body in rivers down my face
I had hoped my own tears would drown me
"Ungumfazi into oyiyo!"[1]
A reminder
Not because I had forgotten that I was a woman
But to further assert their patriarchal entitlement over every woman's virtue
A slut if she gives it up
Frigid if she doesn't
And whether or not consent is given
Misogyny lays claim to it

They barely noticed the life escape my flesh
They discarded my lifeless body like trash
Because what use do wild animals have for empty carcasses
It was my mother who discovered the dead body
Under that street light
The one that has never worked quite right
A mere glance away from the safety of home.

SINAZO SOMHLAHLO
*Sesotho-English translation by Vuyokazi Ngemntu*

---

[1] What you are is a woman!

## a revolution

i remember
when i decided to sleep
in the middle of the bed.
it was an act of rebellion
a revolution.
there was no
my side
and his side.
it was all mine
and on some nights
i would lie
limbs spread
and on others
i would hold myself
gently
but fiercely
in the smallest ball
and slowly
i started to reclaim my space
gently but fiercely.

    CAITLIN SPRING

# MINE WILL BE OF AFRICA

I am not of Africa,
but I am of the soil,
of this soul.

I hanker for the teachings
of tales of oppression,
with the local lagers clenched
in my foreign-feeling fingers.

I hark back to the odysseys
over battlegrounds
of unpopular warfare,
long forgotten.

I long for the meat and wohobe
untouched by Western corporation,
feasted upon with
grandfather and formidable friends.

The voyage and hang about
will evermore be concurrent with
the anxious outlander
sitting in the council meeting.

The insect repelled room
on the banks of Zambezi,
and the vibrancy and halcyon
of subcontinent cities.

I call to mind continuously
the shaking of the hand
of the sons
of autocratic charisma.

My pale pink face against
the fire,
of a land at the breast,
of a continent convoluted
by colonial clasping.

I will make mine,
future and issue,
of this red and sandy earth,
of Africa.

        DAVID C STEYN

# EVEN BIRDS
*For Faith*

We arrive in Cambridge
after a long night's flight:
eighteen twenty-somethings
with a hangover of Africa.

What really matters, the man says,
is everyone's comfort.
We wouldn't want anyone
to be out
of place.
Don't ask and don't confess
potential transgressions.
This is a tour, after all.

So I keep clear of the line,
sick, tight with my truth.

Faith is still too
but later that night
she knocks on my door
and cries for skin
she's never been in.
These queer
constructs: towers cut
on ancestors' backs.

We discuss spectrums
of shame.

Late dawn is lilac
phosphorescence crossed
with migrating shadows.
There's no snow, just white ash.

Surely the others see;
they must sense our bent.
Even birds know silence
is also an answer.

        CAITLIN STOBIE

# REFUGEE

You whorl into me
your seashell self
in the ocean of my bed
I hold you hard against my heart
awake
when I should be sleeping

Because all I see
is that small boy
lifeless on the beach
wearing the shoes
his mother chose that morning
– his best –
put on to greet his new life

                LOUELLA SULLIVAN

# THEATRE OF HEARTS
*Hamilton Naki, 1926–2005*

Remember Hamilton who rose from gardener
to cleaner of animal cages
to teacher-with-no-training of students and physicians
to black laboratory assistant of Christiaan
the white heart surgeon.
*Technically, Hamilton is a better surgeon than I am.*
*Some operations I cannot do.*

Confined to a back room
he removes, inserts and stitches livers
jugulars and hearts into the flesh of a giraffe
and many dogs and pigs:
*Animals Only.*

See him cross the courtyard of Groote Schuur.
He carries a box of hearts for his surgeon
and enters a lift:
*Non-Whites Only.*

Today in the Christiaan Barnard hospital
I hear a girl in the ward of damaged hearts call:
*Mamy! Mamy!*
Listen to the voice of the black doctor
back from theatre
moving bed-to-bed on his rounds
to hear each desolate
human heart.

ELIZABETH TREW

# STHANDWA SAM'

Sthandwa sam' Umanginawe ngikhohlwa zonke izinsizi
   zam'
Bazamile ukungikhohlis' abangani bam'
Bangitshela ngendlela ongayilungelanga ngayo impilo yam'
Ngabatshela, uma bengakwazi ukungeseka ezinqumeni
   zam'
Mabayishiye phansi impilo yam'

Ngosuku lwethu lokuqala sithandana,
Ngangingazi nokuthi ngizobatshela kanjani ekhaya
Ukuthi sengimtholile umaqondana wam'
Futhi uyawujabulisa umphefumulo wam'

Ngawutshela umndeni wam'
Ukuthi ulungise phela siyeza isithandwa sam'
Umjulisi wenhliziyo yam'
Uza nje uphethe izinkomo zam'

Sthandwa sam' athi amaningi amantombazane esigodini
   sam'
Wakheth' ukuba nam'
Ntandokazi yam'
Ngiyakuthembisa, uma wena unami
Uzokhohlwa nokuthi awusenabo abazali.

Safika ekhaya isithandwa sam'
Siphethe izinkomo zam'
Zaxoxwa izindaba zelobolo.
Kikiki! Ngathathwa mina kwa Khumalo,
Mtungwa ,Mbulaz' omnyama

Ngabashiya ababesondelene nam'
Ngayohlala nesithandwa sam'
Bathi befikile bazongivakashela abangani bam'
Ngabaxosha emzini wam'

Ngasixoxela isithandwa sam'
Ukuthi ngibaxoshile abangani bam'
Sangibuza ukuthi kungani?
Ngasitshela isithandwa sam'
Ukuthi abakwazanga ukungeseka ezinqumeni zam'

Lwafika usuku lwethu olukhulu,
Kwakukhona ngisho ogogo nomkhulu.
Ngibonga umdali wam'
Ngokungilethela isithandwa sam'

Masithokoze sthandwa sam'
Ngoba Mina nawe siqeda iminyaka.
Akekho ozongena phakathi kwethu
Nkosi busisa loluthando lwethu

Ngihlala ngenamile emzini wam'
Phela singiphethe kahle isithandwa sam'
Ubaba wezingane zam'
Umsizi wempilo yam'

Bahlala benama omakhelwane umasixabana,
Phela sixabana nje, siyathandana.

Phela sathembisana ukuthi kuyo yonke into sizokwesekana
Mbulaz' wam omnyama.
Sthandwa sam' ngiyabonga ngokungeseka empilweni yam'
Ukube awuzange ungene empilweni yam'
Ngabe ngiwundinga sithebeni.
Uyilesifo engingafuni ukusilapha emzimbeni wam'
Mesuli wezinyembezi emehlweni ami.
Ngiyabonga sthandwa sam'
Mbulaz' wam omnyama

LESEGO TSOHO

# MY LOVE

My love when I am with you I forget all my sufferings
Many people tried to lie to me
Telling me about how you are not the right person for me
I told them if they can't stand by my decisions
They better leave my life

On our first day as lovers
I didn't know how I was going to break the news at home
That I have found my partner
The one who makes my soul happy

I told my family
To prepare for my lover is coming
The one who makes my heart happy
He comes with my herd of cattle

My love many girls in my neighbourhood say,
You chose to be mine
My love
I promise if you are with me
You will forget that you are an orphan

My lover arrived at my homestead
With my herd of cattle
Discussions for lobola got underway
Kikiki, the Khumalos took me home
*Mtungwa, Mbulaz omnyama*

I left those who used to be close to me
And went to live with my lover

My friends said they came to visit
I chased them away from my home

I am telling my lover
That I chased my friends
He asked me why
I told my lover
That they never supported my decisions

Our big day arrived
There was young and old people
I thank my creator
For giving me my lover

Let us be happy my love
For we both spent a long time
No one will come between us
Please Lord bless our love

I live well in my home
For my lover treats me well
Father of my children
The helper of my life

The neighbours like it when we fight
But we fight because we love each other
And we promised each other that we will always support
    each other
My dark Mbulaz

I thank you my lover for standing by me in my life
If you didn't become part of my life
I would be lost
You are a disease in my body I don't want to treat
My shoulder to cry on
Thank you my love
My dark Mbulaz

> *Translated from the isiZulu original – Lesego Tsoho's*
> *'Sthandwa sam'' – by Goodenough Mashego*

# NGIYABONGA MAMA

Sthandwa senhliziyo yam'
Uthando lwakho angazi ngilufanise nani. Ungihole kwaze kwaba yinamuhla.
Ngihamba endleleni elungile nje, nguwe.
Nkosi busisa umawami,
Onothando olubanzi.
Ngiyabonga mama

Wathola nje ukuthi ngiyeza,
Awuzange ucabange ukungibulala.
Kwezinye izinsuku ngangikushuka,
Waqinisela ngoba wazi ukuthi uphethe isikhulu.
Nkosi busisa umawami,
Onothando olubanzi.
Ngiyabonga mama.

Ungibekezelile ngisemncane,
Nanoma ngangiwubatefile.
Ngoba ngiyintandokazi yakho.
Nanoma ngingekho endlini,
Awukhathazeki ngoba uyazi ngiphephile.
Nkosi busisa umawami,
Onothando olubanzi.
Ngiyabonga mama.

Wangishushuzela ngephimbo elimtoti,
Ngemilolozelo yezingane.
Wangigoba ngisemanzi.
Ngiyazilonda njal' izimfundiso zakho.
Ziyohlala zihlel' enhlizweni yam'

Ngoba uyintandokazi yam'
Nkosi busisa umawami,
Onothando olubanzi.
Ngiyabonga mama.

Wawungiphethe okweqanda.
Wangixoxela ngezindaba ezimnandi zenkosi yethu.
Ngiyisabe futhi ngiyikhonze njalo.
Nkosi busisa umawami,
Onothando olubanzi.
Ngiyabonga mama.

Awukaze wangidukisa,
Uma ngikhala, uyangithulisa.
Awu Kodwa Jesu ! Ngenzeni engaka ukuze ngithole
    uthando olungaka?
Umangikude nawe,
Ngicabanga ngawe, inhliziyo yam' iyadukluza.
Nkosi busisa umawami,
Onothando olubanzi.
Ngiyabonga mama.

Ukudla kwakho kwehla ngesiphundu.
Ngathi ukupheka wakufundela enyuvesi.
Ngiyamamatheka njalo umangikubona weneme.
Isihleko sakho singithinta emanonini.
Nkosi busisa umawami,
Onothando olubanzi.
Ngiyabonga mama.

Kuningi engingakusho ngawe.
Phezu kwakho konje,
Ngibonga uthando onginika lona mihla namalanga.
Yingakho ngihleli entendeni yesandla sakho.
Kunzima ukuwuvala umlomo ngawo.
Nkosi busisa umawami,
Onothando olubanzi.
Ngiyabonga mama.

              LESEGO TSOHO

# THANK YOU MAMA

The love of my heart
Your love is incomparable
You took care of me until today
Because of you I walk in a path of goodness,
Please Lord bless my Mama
Who is full of love
Thank you Mama

When you knew I was coming
You never contemplated abortion
Sometimes I would cause you morning sickness
You stood strong 'cause you knew you carried a giant
Please Lord bless my Mom
Thank you Mama

You tolerated me since I was young
Even when I behaved spoiled
Because I am your daughter
Even when I am absent from home
You worry not 'cause you know I am safe
Please Lord bless my Mom
Who is full of love
Thank you Mama

You cuddled me on your warm chest
With lullabies
You mended me while still wet
I forever treasure your guidance
They will forever reside in my heart
Because you are the love of my heart

Lord please bless my Mom
Who is full of love
Thank you Mama

You handled me with care
You preached me the good news of our Lord
I respect and fear the Lord
Lord please bless my Mom
Who is full of love
Thank you Mama

You never misled me
When I cry you wipe my tears
Lord Jesus, what have I done to deserve such love
When I am far from you
I think of you I think of you my heart skips a beat
Please Lord bless my Mom
Who is full of love
Thank you Mama

Your food tastes like no other
As if you learnt culinary skills at university
I smile everytime I see you happy
Your laugh tickles me inside
Lord please bless my Mom
Who is full of love
Thank you Mama

There's a lot I say about you
Above all
I thank the love you give me everyday
That's why I reside in the tent of your hand
It's difficult to not talk about you
Lord please bless my Mom
Who is full of love
Thank you Mama

> *Translated from the isiZulu original – Lesego Tsoho's*
> *'Ngiyabonga Mama' – by Goodenough Mashego*

# IN MY CUPBOARD

In my cupboard hang clothes I wear often
And others I have almost forgotten
Still I keep them for an occasion
Where they may come in handy
The clothes I love are worn out quickly
Those I never wear last
I wonder if my favourites
Would rather be ignored and live longer
It is safe in the cupboard
Where there is nothing to stretch them
To pull at their stitches
But when they come out
They go places
And feel the warmth of touch
True, they may fade and fray more quickly
And risk being torn every day
But at least they will serve their purpose
They will know what life is like
That there is so much more to do than hang around

TROYDON WAINWRIGHT

# A WEDDING POEM

Love has done this
Love has stitched these two together
And made something new
Love has bound threads once loose
And made their fabric stronger
From now on each will rest on the other
When stretched they will draw closer
From now on they are the same line
What has come so far will go further
And intertwine itself into the great design

> TROYDON WAINWRIGHT

# INVESTMENT RETURNS

The rim of the garbage bin
presses hard into her ribs
as she invests a stubby arm deep
into the market of others' excess
in search of returns on her invested effort.
'Old Woman Bent Over Garbage Bin,'
the caption of this photo will read.

Upon my enquiry she recounts her profits:
'A half-eaten sandwich or banana,
sometimes I find money,
sometimes I even find jewellery.'
Like a Wall Street banker, proud
of her track record of gains,
she smiles gleefully, exposing
her purple toothless gums.
But her glow immediately vanishes
as her humanity returns;
her head drops, leaking pure white hair
from her bright-coloured doek:
'More and more,' she continues glumly,
'I find little babies.'

'Who abandons these babies?' I puke,
earning her derisive reply:
'Obviously its poor frightened mothers,
or capitalists and politicians.'
'Obviously,' I stutter,
as she continues investing
before the markets close.

ATHOL WILLIAMS

# VISIT AT TEA TIME

I killed a man, she says, her memories hanging
heavy, like long thick black braids from her head
hung low. Her demons have sunk their claws
into her cheeks, her sins trapped in dark bags of pain
hanging beneath her eyes, eyes that look as though
they once knew how to smile.

What are you in for? I'd asked the eighteen-year-old
drowning in her torment and oversized blue uniform
sitting in a Pollsmoor prison cell, her small frame
drawn as tightly into itself as her horror will allow.

My wife was not happy for me to come here, visiting
a murderer. She fired a barrage of fearful questions:
bars, will there be bars or glass between you and her?
Will a guard be present? What if something goes wrong?
Why can't someone else go? It's just for a cup of tea
and a prayer, I assured her. There is no safety barrier,
I am sitting face to face with a killer, someone who
has taken a life, broken commandments while
the rest of us broke promises. She doesn't look like
a murderer, but what face does a murderer wear?

Thou shalt not kill, I remind myself, the words roll
around my mind as I roll the pen around in my pocket,
my weapon of defence in case I need one.
There is never a reason to kill, my morality whispers,
we have given her the justice she deserves.

I stabbed him in the neck, she continues, unprompted,

snapping me back from my righteousness. Her spirit
seems to recoil as she pukes the words; she looks
shocked, as though hearing of her crime anew, like
a young soldier just awaking to her role in an unjust war.
I reported every time, every time I was raped, she sobs.
Everyone knows, she says, with a sadness that makes
my body quake, cold. It happens to all the girls
in the township; even if we report it, even if we scream,
no one helps. When it happened the seventh time,
I killed him, I killed the man who did it.

The seventh time! I scream in silence.

I don't want to go free, she says softly, after a pause;
someone has to pay for our sins, her hard eyes fixed
intensely on mine. When you're born in the shadows
you never find light, she says. Who makes the shadows?
her voice tails off. Who makes the shadows? I repeat.

I know who makes the shadows.

Like a hammer to my forehead, chaos explodes. I hear
loud echoes all around, heavy steel smashing against
heavy steel, doors banging, anguished screams, barking
guards. I hear eerie chatter like tree leaves fist-fighting
in the wind, tongues reciting sins. I can't find comfort
anywhere in my chair. Where's the tea? It is tea time
dammit, but I've got no tea, where's the fucking tea!
I leave in a hurry,
no time for prayer,

just glad to be outside.
I rush off to find some tea,
or maybe something stronger.

    ATHOL WILLIAMS

## missing

fragments of pure refrain
lift above and beyond
the wail of the wind
notes rise in sad
crescendo
straining
to reach
the apex
to arc
i
n
mid air
to fall
slowly
achingly
driving a knife
between the ribs
spilling notes onto the sand
to swell in the flow of salt water
returning a small boy to the beach

SUE WOODWARD

# Afterword

"A diminutive figure physically, only 5 feet 2 inches tall, Solomon Tshekisho Plaatje was in every other respect a giant. He possessed a formidable intellect, and was a man of integrity, wit and great charm. A committed Christian, teetotaller, champion of the oppressed, inveterate letter-writer, author, journalist, interpreter, politician, globetrotter and devoted family man, Plaatje stands out as one of the most remarkable South Africans of his time."

Perhaps these words by Maureen Rall in the introduction of her book *Peaceable Warrior – The Life and Times of Sol T. Plaatje* explain the awe with which Plaatje and his work are viewed, almost 85 years since his death. The Sol Plaatje European Union Poetry Award and Anthology is a very important way to pay homage to this humble man of letters.

Sol Plaatje believed in the power of the written word, and poets do and exemplify that too. The role played by poets such as Mongane Wally Serote and Don Mattera from the 1970s, and the apartheid regime's response to their writing, attest to the power of words, written and/or spoken.

About a century ago – in 1916 – when Plaatje penned *Native Life in South Africa* he did so with the main intention of appealing to the moral senses of the "sympathetic reader". At that time what he called "a very strange law" had been passed and the South African Native was to become "a pariah in the land of his birth". With words as his weapons against the mighty Union of South Africa parliament which had just passed the Natives Land Act of 1913, Plaatje set out to write. "Mine is but a sincere narrative of a melancholy situation, in which with all its shortcomings, I have endeavoured to describe the difficulties of the South African natives under a very strange law, so as most readily to be understood by the sympathetic reader." The book was well received by the British public – it was published in London – as well as getting the attention of the parliament in South Africa. Plaatje's dedication to writing as his contribution to, among others, the battle against the Natives Land Act, as well as the response to *Native Life* in particular, is an indication of the role as well as the power of the written word in society.

But Plaatje fought, using the might of the pen and imagination, the struggles of his time. What are the struggles of our time as read in this anthology? In Plaatje's time the affairs of the "South African Native" were deliberated upon and decided in a parliament that thought of him a problem or rather "a question", the land was taken away and there was no constitution like the current Act 108 of 1996. The South African "Native" was a mere provider of labour.

Some of the issues are still here today. There might actually be more. Or less. But there is a multiplicity, a mishmash of issues that poets and writers of today are dealing with. In this anthology these issues range from Dorian Haarhof's haunting poem about father-son relationships to Fiona Khan who talks about the beauty that refuses to go away in the face of all kinds of weather. Then Musawenkosi Khanyile draws our attention to the lines that are drawn to separate the rich from the poor in his poem "Class". He paints a powerful yet haunting image of a society where "lines" put everybody into classes, where they "belong".

In "There's A Me That's Still Not Free" Portia Mabaso tells us why, as Chimamanda Ngozi Adichie said, we should all be feminists and bring down patriarchy with all we have. *"There's a me that's still, like the bird of Maya, caged|Caged and singing with a fearful trill the song of freedom,"* she writes.

Also very evident in Plaatje's legacy is his deep love and respect for mother-tongue. Apart from the newspapers – *Koranta ea Becoana*, *Tsala ea Becoana* and *Tsala ea Batho* – that he published in an African language and English, Plaatje also wrote the *Sechuana Reader* between May 1915 and September 1916 with linguist Daniel Jones at the University College of London. This was, according to Jones, "a complete and accurate record of pronunciation of this extraordinarily interesting language". He was referring to Setswana, Plaatje's first language. In 1916 he published *Sechuana Proverbs and the European Equivalents*. Then there were translations of William Shakespeare's works: *Comedy of Errors* to *Diphosho-Phosho* and *Julius Caesar* to *Dintšhontšho Tsa Bo-Juliuse Kesara*.

Plaatje's commitment to African languages also comes out in, among many, a letter published in *Umteteleli wa Bantu* edition of 2 April 1932, in which he is charging on white government officials of dipping their fingers where they should not. "It would appear that the gentlemen who control the Education Departments are definitely after a parody of the Native language to suit the tongues of Europeans and not of Natives." He went on to add that "the Native language they regard as a plaything for the mental exercise of European students". This was his seriousness about African languages, not just his mother-tongue. There cannot be a better tribute to Sol Plaatje than this bravura as displayed through a variety of African languages by the likes of Tsietsi Mokhele in "Gauta o ja batho", Thabiso Mofokeng in "Ho thaba ba ileng", Moses Mtileni in "Laniwani" and Amanda Nodada in "Ilizwe lam".

Plaatje's sentiments were echoed decades later by

Kenyan Ngũgĩ wa Thiong'o in *Decoloninsing the Mind*: "Language carries culture, and culture carries, particularly, through orature and literature, the entire body of values by which we come to perceive ourselves and our place in the world."

*Sabata-mpho Mokae*
*Sol Plaatje University, Kimberley*
*September 2016*

Sabata-mpho Mokae writes in English and Setswana (a southern African language). He is the author of a biography, *The Story of Sol T Plaatje*, a youth novella *Dikeledi* [Tears] and a poetry collection *Escaping Trauma*. His first novel, *Ga Ke Modisa* [I'm Not My Brother's Keeper] won the M-Net Literary Award for Best Novel in Setswana as well as the M-Net Film Award in 2013. The same book has since been prescribed as study material at the North West University as well as the Central University of Technology. Mokae also won the South African Literary Award (literary journalism category) in 2011. His short story "Down Sol Plaatje Drive" was performed on theatre stage during the Global Express in Iowa City, USA in 2014. His latest book, *Kanakotsame: In My Times*, a collection of English short stories, was launched in 2015. In September/October 2015 he was a writer of the month in Ghana. He holds a Master of Arts degree in Creative Writing from Rhodes University where he is currently a PhD candidate. In 2014 Mokae was a writer-in-residence at the University of Iowa. He is a creative writing lecturer at the Sol Plaatje University in Kimberley, South Africa.

# Biographies

**Caroline F Archer** grew up on a farm in the Orange Free State. She loves the outdoors and riding on horseback. Caroline was the Dux Scholar at a small-town Free State school. She studied languages at the University of the Free State and passed with distinction. Her studies included Afrikaans, English, German, French, Philosophy, Psychology as well as Sociology.

Her research of mainly Dutch poets won her with the Tafelberg Award for Excellence in Afrikaans and Dutch. She devotes her leisure time to mentally and physically handicapped children. She works as a radio broadcaster, creates tapes for the blind and works from home as a translator and editor.

**Mutinta Bbenkele** is a spoken word artist from Johannesburg. Having been born in Botswana, raised by Zambian parents (traditionally), living in South Africa from the age of three years old, Mutinta has quite a story to tell. Mutinta has been performing her poetry since 2009 and her eight-year commitment to spoken word is only a glimpse into the admiration she has for poetry. Priding her self in her story-telling format of poetry, Mutinta has been to over four countries to perform her work.

**Tanisha Bhana** is a self-trained artist based in Johannesburg, South Africa. Influenced by her profession as an attorney in the financial services global markets industry, her connection to her ancient heritage, and projects in marginalised communities in South Africa, she claims to act as a medium for the places that we inhabit.

She has participated in various solo and curated group exhibitions both in South Africa and internationally and held discussions and displayed artwork on the topics of rebirth, transformation and decomposition and worked on collaborative projects and performance-dialogues on war, women and the human spirit.

**Zéwande Bk. Bhengu** is a poet from the Eastern Cape currently working in Johannesburg, Gauteng. He is a multi-award-winning poet who has most recently been featured in the *Mail & Guardian* 200 Young South Africans list as well as being one of the opening acts for the International AIDS Conference held in Durban. He has been featured on multiple TV shows showcasing his work and has also performed all through South Africa.

**Rene Bohnen** has been published in various anthologies, which include *Die Groot Verseboek*, *Die heel mooiste Afrikaanse liefdesgedigte*, *Electric Juice* and *As die son kom oogknip*. Her debut, *Spoorsny*, was published in 2000 and was followed in 2011 by *In die niks al om*, published by LAPA Uitgewers. Rene holds a Master's degree in Creative Writing and an Honours degree in English.

**Kathryn Clare Botes** is a dreamer, residing in South Africa. Although by day she is a manager, her heart belongs to the arts, with a passion for writing in particular. She found a love and talent for writing from a young age, enjoying both prose and poetry, but with a strength in the latter.

**Dianne Case** is a published author of books mostly for children and has won several awards for her youth novels.

She loves reading poetry and writes poetry for herself and has not had any poetry published yet.

**Christine Coates** is a poet and writer from Cape Town. She has a Master's degree in Creative Writing from the University of Cape Town. Her poems were selected for the *Sol Plaatje European Union Poetry Anthology* 2011–2015, and Best "New" African Poets 2015 Anthology. Her debut collection *Homegrown*, published in 2014 by Modjaji Books, received an honourable mention from the Glenna Luschei Prize.

Her short stories have been highly commended; 'The Cat's Wife' in *Adults Only*, the Short.Sharp.Stories anthology 2014, and 'How We Look Now' in *Water*, the Short Story Day Africa anthology 2015. She recently participated in the inaugural Rutanang Book Fair in Potchefstroom.

**Bella (B-Lyrical) Cox** is a spoken word slam and performance poet, vocalist and media creator. She has been performing in and around Gauteng since early 2014 and is a WordnSound Queen of the Mic as well as a perfect poem nominee. She has won multiple amateur slam competitions around Gauteng and has also showcased in Durban.

B-Lyrical is best known for her raw, truth-telling poetic style, quirky love poems and controversial socio-political pieces.

Since graduating from the University of Pretoria in 2016 she has been working full time as a performer both on stage and camera and she hopes to publish her first anthology by the end of 2016.

**Lise Day** has recently retired to Hout Bay after forty years of teaching English, most recently at the Nelson Mandela

University. She is a member of the 'Pleached Poetry' writing circle and regularly attends and enjoys workshops with Finuala Dowling. Her short stories have been published in the English National Curriculum textbook and in periodicals and books. She has had poems published in *Carapace*, two editions of the *Sol Plaatje European Union Poetry Anthology*, *New Contrast* and online in Aerodrome.

**Graham Dukas** is a business consultant, corporate coach and retired architect. His poetry explores territory that ranges from the serious to the absurd, often dismantling the familiar with a subversive wit and unexpected logic. He has two self-published poetry chapbooks to his name. He lives in Cape Town with his wife and a sprinkling of cats.

**Elaine Edwards** is a poet, dancer, artist and free spirit who lives in Melkbosstrand on the West Coast. She loves to travel, especially in South Africa, where she is inspired by the landscape, voices of the past, wild weather and passionate conversation.

**Cornelia Smith-Fick (Connie Fick)**, also known as Colleen Lynn, is a South African writer. She has just completed a Master's degree in Creative Writing at Rhodes University. A nurse by profession, she worked for a number of years as the editor of a monthly primary health care magazine, and has been a freelance writer for *Takalani Sesame* (radio and TV) since its inception in 2000. Her poems and short stories have been published in various magazines.

**Tshepo Gaerupe** is an entrepreneur, poet and motivational speaker. He is passionate about language. He hosts empowerment seminars and other events.

**Nobuntu Gantana** can best be described as passionate, dedicated, hardworking and committed. From a small village in East London in the Eastern Cape, she is currently working at the Department of Sports, Recreation, Arts and Culture as an Assistant Director: Special Programmes Unit in Grahamstown. As part of her work and in her personal capacity she mentors young girls and equips them with life skills for both their personal and professional development. She is fascinated by languages and has a great love for reading and writing. She is fluent in isiXhosa, English and Afrikaans.

**Sarah Godsell** is an historian and poet. Born in Johannesburg in 1985, her heart is in this city. She has been writing since she can remember, and she has been performing since 2009. She has been published nationally and internationally and has performed on stages such as SANAA Africa, Shift on SABC, and Poetry in the Air on SAFM. In 2016 she published her first full collection of poetry entitled *Seaweed Sky*. Although often pulled down, she consistently chooses up.

**Dorian Haarhoff** is a poet (seven collections), story-teller, mentor and speaker. A former professor of English at the University of Namibia, he is passionate about developing innate creativity and imagination. Dorian believes in the power of images to create new realities. He has been a participating poet at Poetry Africa, SA and presented at the International Poetry Festival in Colombia, South America.

He has recorded a poetry CD. Dorian's wordshops are based on his text *The Writer's Voice: A Workbook for Writers in Africa*. He currently lives in Somerset West, swimming in the sea and hiking in the mountains.

**Kerry Hammerton** has published poetry in various journals and anthologies in South Africa and the UK, most recently *Hallelujah for 50ft Women* (Bloodaxe Books:2015). She has two collections, *The Lies I told You* (Modjaji: 2010) and *The Weather Report* (2014). Kerry has a Master's degree in Creative Writing from Rhodes University.

**Jay Heale** has spent the last nearly 50 years in South Africa, now living in Overberg. Jay has been a teacher, and has worked in the world of books as a reader, author, editor, researcher and reviewer.

**Tracey (Khadija) Heeger** is a Cape Town performance poet. Her work has been characterised as stark and unapologetic. In 2013 Modjaji Books published her debut collection of poems, *Beyond the Delivery Room*. She has performed her poetry as multi-media theatrical pieces in collaboration with soundscape artists Khoikonnexion and Ncebakazi Mnukwana. Her work continues to be relevant, sharp and unafraid.

**Heidi Elisabeth Henning** attended Roedean School where she was awarded the English Essay Prize. She obtained a Bachelor's degree in Law and Psychology from Wits University, and a Master of Science in Creative Writing from Edinburgh University. She has been frequently published in *New Contrast* literary journal and on Litnet.

**Thapelo Hlongwane**, a theatre and performance student at the University Of Cape Town, is well known as Naked Soul in the Arts fraternity. A spoken word artist, founding member of the Tongue Twisters collective, a storyteller, an actor and a theatre maker, he has been involved in quite a number of productions and performances. He co-wrote and co-directed *A man died that night: people of the sky, an excerpt* (2016) by the Tongue Twisters collective at the Alexander Bar and Theatre for Play Things and in the past few years has been making a name for himself in various poetry stages.

**Siphokazi Jonas** is a writer, performer and poet, based in Cape Town, South Africa. She holds a Bachelors degree in English and Drama, and a Master's degree in English Literature from the University of Cape Town. As a performance poet she has featured in numerous events around the country. As a budding theatre-maker, she recently staged her first multi-genre production, *Around the Fire*, at the Artscape Theatre. In 2015, Jonas was the curator of Poetica, the poetry component of the Open Book Festival. She works as a teaching assistant in the English Department at UCT, and occasionally lectures on South African poetry.

**Fiona Khan** is an internationally published award-winning writer. She is also an academic and environmentalist. She has been writing and has been published since 1992, with poems and short stories published in anthologies and literary magazines around the world. Her literary romance novel *Reeds of Wrath* is set in the time of Indian indentured labour in KZN. She has been one of South Africa's leading children's writers with more than 10 titles to her name. Her books appear in the schools catalogue and have set a precedence in HIV/AIDS, emotional intelligence and language and literacy in South Africa.

**Musawenkosi Khanyile** is a 25-year-old poet, born and raised in Nseleni township. His poetry has appeared in *New Coin*, *Kalahari Review*, *The Sol Plaatje European Union Poetry Anthology*, Aerodrome and other literally journals.

**Lara Kirsten** is a pianist and performance poet. She holds a Bachelor's degree in Music (Honours) from the University of Pretoria. As a solo pianist and accompanist for singers and instrumentalists, she performs all over South Africa. As a poet, she has performed in the Netherlands and at various venues in South Africa. Lara has performed at the Wakkerstroom Music Festival, the McGregor Poetry Festival, the AfrikaBurn Festival in the Tankwa Karoo, and the Woordfees in Stellenbosch. She belongs to the Eastern Cape poetry group, Ecca, and has recorded a CD of her own poetry.

**Lynne Kloot** is a long-time member of a poetry workshop run by Finuala Dowling, to whom she attributes her growth as a poet. She has been by turns a teacher, journalist and editor.

**Nomnikelo Komanisi** was born in Stellenbosch, Western Cape. She used to be a high school teacher in Cape Town, but started as a language practitioner at the University of Western Cape, at Iilwimi Sentrum. She works as a language practitioner in the South African National Parliament, in Cape Town. She loves what is connected to love of culture, which is why she loves writing – because language goes with culture. Reading opens her mind and writing eases her mind and heals her soul. Whatever she has for her personal development or to equip others, she does in writing.

**Portia Mabaso**, also known as laposche, is a poet and aspiring songwriter. Her influence transcends gender, colour or religion. Her poetry centres around identity; its struggles and glories, self-love and transcendence. She fell in love with poetry after reading the likes of Zakes Mda, Elizabeth Barret Browning, Lebo Mashile, Maya Angelou, Rumi and many others.

**Songeziwe Mahlangu** was born in Alice. He holds a Master's degree in Creative Writing from Rhodes University. In 2013, he published his debut novel, *Penumbra*.

**Patrick Maitland** was born in 1932 in Port Elizabeth. He went to boarding school in Grahamstown and then studied at Rhodes for BSc and BCom degrees. Afterwards, he worked in Cape Town before starting his own business, which he ran for 27 years before retiring. He has been writing poetry for the last 15 years.

**Maishe Maponya** is a playwright, theatre director, poet and cultural activist. He was the founder and director of the performing arts group, Bahumutsi. His plays include *Gangsters*, *Dirty Work*, *Bušang Meropa* and *The Hungry Earth*. His other works in theatre include performances based on the stories of Sol Plaatje and Steve Biko. Maponya has a Master's degree from Leeds University, UK and was a lecturer in Drama at the University of the Witwatersrand in Johannesburg. He is currently working on a musical show entitled *The Ghost of Tzaneen*.

**Charles Marriott** was a high school educator for 16 years, now a coach and soft skill facilitator running a youth leadership NPO. He has been writing poetry since he was 20. At 20, he wrote badly. He is gradually getting better.

**Kela Griot Maswabi** is a human becoming; a curious soul that is always finding and losing herself in words. She is a scribe, an evolving creative, finding expression in freelance writing, poetry, prose and scriptwriting. You'll find her nestled between jazz and ink.

**Zongezile Theophilus Matshoba** is from Mdantsane, but lives and works in Grahamstown, Eastern Cape. Over the past 20 years, he has practised as a freelance journalist and a teacher. He is the co-founder of Inkcubeko Media Productions. His main interests include photography, video production, online media, stage-play production and short-story writing.

His isiXhosa and English writings narrate the humour and hardships of township and rural life, and interrogate whether it is yet uhuru in people's livelihood.

**Katise Mawela** is a freelance journalist and poet based in Johannesburg. He also works as a professional nurse. His poems have appeared in different publications, including the *Sol Plaatje European Union Poetry Anthology* twice.

**Ongezwa Mbele** is 32-year-old applied theatre practitioner, born in Cape Town and raised in Durban. She is currently working in Norway for a year doing prison theatre. She is easily moved by the arts.

**Marthé Mcloud** was born in Stellenbosch. She received her Master's degree in Social Work in 1989, and has worked as a social worker in the Strand since.

In her free time she writes poetry, some of which has been published on LitNet. In 2016 she won second place in a national poetry competition – Bloemfonteinse Skrywersvereniging. One of her exhibitions, 'Onse Mense 2', about the artist Marie Stander, was included in Wordfees 2016 in Stellenbosch.

**Thabiso Mofokeng** was born in Qwaqwa, Free State. He is a professional writer, literary and language practitioner. He facilitates creative writing workshops in poetry and prose. Some of his books are prescribed by the Department of Education for grade 8 and grade 10. He appears in various anthologies and journals in Sesotho and English. He published a collection of Sesotho poetry in 2015. He completed his Master's degree in Creative Writing with distinctions at Rhodes University in 2015. He is currently studying towards his PhD in Literature at the University of the Western Cape.

**Maneo Refiloe Mohale** is a writer and poet. Her work has appeared in various print and online publications, including *Jalada*, *HOLAA!*, *The Beautiful Project*, *From the Root Zine*, *Mail & Guardian*, and *Expound* magazine. She is the 2016 Bitch Media Global Feminism Writing Fellow and writes on various topics, including race, media, queerness, survivorship, language, history and silliness.

**Tsietsi Mokhele** is a language activist who mainly writes in Sesotho with a view to promote and preserve the language. He is currently working on his debut collection of Sesotho short stories and poems. Some of his poems have been published by ITCH online journal (Issue 3 and 4), *Poetry Potion, Love letters to My Child*, and 2015 *Sol Plaatje European Union Poetry Anthology*.

**George Momogos** lives with his wife Anne in suburbia in Durban, on the east coast of South Africa, where taxis don't stop for red lights, strays, and the blue-light brigade. He is a fledgling writer and a blogger editor at "Working for Customers". He lectures as an independent contractor on a number of business management courses at a private university and is continually surprised by how much he loves it. All this while managing his online learning business.

**Jackie Mondi** is a black South African woman who is a writer, poet and teacher. She strives to harness the power of the written word to change people's lives. Her writing has been published in *The Sol Plaatje European Union Poetry Anthology* (volumes 1, 2 and 4), *Face of the Spirit – Illuminating a century of essays by South African Women*, *So Much To Tell Vol. 2 – An Anthology of South African women writing*, *Agenda*, *The SA Labour Bulletin*, *Wrapped* magazine; and quoted in the 2009 Budget Speech. Jackie lives in Johannesburg with her husband Lumkile and son Vuyo.

**Nedine Moonsamy** is a senior lecturer in the English Literature department at the University of Pretoria. She is currently writing a monograph on nostalgia and nationalism in contemporary South African fiction and launching a research project on science fiction in Africa.

**Moses Mtileni** is the author of two collections of poetry, *U ya va rungula*, and *When the Moon Goes to Rest*; and a novel, *Mpimavayeni*. His poems and short stories have appeared in several anthologies and journals, including *Asymptote*, *Timbila*, *Botsotso* and *Ons Klyntji*. He holds three Master's degrees from Wits and Rhodes universities. He was born at Nkuri-Tomu village, in Giyani.

Born and raised in Daveyton, as a poet and a young writer his greatest highlight so far has been an honour mention in the South African Writers College short story competition.

**Nick Mulgrew** was born in Durban in 1990 to British parents. He is the author of two books: a poetry collection, *The Myth of this Is that We're All in this Together*; and *Stations*, a suite of short fiction. He is the founder and publisher of uHlanga, a poetry press. Nick currently lives in Cape Town.

**Luthando Ncayiyana** is a Margate-born student, currently attending Port Shepstone High School in Port Shepstone, KZN. His writing seeks to explore themes of power, memory and mortality.

**Pamela Newham** worked for many years as a journalist. She has published three children's books and lectures on writing for children and journalism. She lives in Hout Bay.

**Mandla Robert Ngakane** is a 29-year-old pan-African Sowetan. He is a football coach in the local leagues and a writer/poet. He started writing intensely in his teens and has kept at it; although not published, he has taken his writing as a meditating ritual of spiritual health and growth. He finds inspiration in music, books, art and in the suasion of hope in life.

Writer-performer **Vuyokazi Ngemntu** (alias Dejavu Tafari) fuses elements of story-telling, spoken word, physical theatre, song and satire to create performance poetry which lends itself to topics that range from spirituality to intimacy and social commentary. A passionate Afro-optimist, she considers her performance work an extension of her purpose as the healer/trainee sangoma that she currently is. Her recent achievements include an invitation to the Texa International Poetry Festival, where she presided as their International Guest Poet in April of 2016.

**Bomi Njoloza** is a versatile writer, poet and advocate for mother-tongue literacy; a child and student of the universe. Bomi Njoloza arrived on this planet just over two decades ago in the land of silent hills, iminga and scarlet aloes. This child of forgiveness, peace, and laughter molds poetry, speaks and tells stories in more ways than can be understood.

Her poetry anthology, *The Colour of Love*, which was launched in March 2012, includes a foreword by Zakes Mda who had this to say: "Hers is a voice that demands to be heard; a gentle voice, now playful, now plaintive. It is a voice that is sometimes joyful and songful and at other times mournful and soulful. It is a youthful and exuberant voice. A danceful voice. It is never slight, never shrill. It is full-bodied and lovable. This is a voice that is bound to develop stronger and stronger into a major one. One day it will engage multitudes in all continents. Mark my words."

Bomi Njoloza is currently working on her second collection of works, *Shapes of Forgiveness*.

**Amanda Nodada** is a poet, writer, performer and a former radio personality, currently residing in Pretoria.

She studied Performing Arts at Community Arts Project

(2001), followed by a Bachelor's degree in Languages and Communications at the University of the Western Cape (2005).

She has published a poetry book (Isililo, 2010), contributed her work on the following poetry anthologies: *At Truth's Edge* (2011 with other eight poets) and *Ingqaka Yesihobe* (isiXhosa anthology 2012 published by Oxford University Press) and an isiXhosa anthology, *Yagragrama Imbongi*, to be published by Oxford University Press and available later this year. Amanda's work has also been featured on learner's language books currently used at schools.

**Sihle Ntuli** is a South African writer and part-time Master's degree candidate at the School of Languages and Literature at Rhodes University. Since 2009, his poems have been published in *Poetry Potion*, *New Coin*, *New Contrast* and *Ja* magazine, among others. He has also been published in an array of publications such as *Saraba* and *Kalahari Review*.

He has read his poetry at several literature festivals and in 2015 as part of Bakwa's music feature edition, he curated a pan-African playlist in collaboration with *Ja* magazine entitled 'Phola'. In the same year he released his debut anthology of poetry entitled *Stranger* to favourable reviews. In 2016, he contributed an isiZulu translation of Ngugi Wa Thiongo's short story 'The Upright Revolution' – and this was part of the acclaimed Africa-wide translation edition.

**Lazola Pambo** is a South African poet, novelist and essayist.

The majority of his works have been published in *The Kalahari Review*, *Aerodrome*, *New Coin*, *Nomad's Choir*, *Black Magnolias Literary Journal*, *BlazeVOX*, LitNet, and

*Indiana Voice Journal*. Other works of his are forthcoming in the *Sentinel Literary Quarterly*.

You can follow him on Twitter @LPambo.

**Jim Pascual Agustin** writes and translates poetry in Filipino and English. He grew up in the Philippines and moved to Cape Town, South Africa in 1994. His most recent books are published by the University of Santo Tomas Publishing House in Manila: *Baha-bahagdang Karupukan* (2011, poems in Filipino), *Alien to Any Skin* (2011, poems in English), *Kalmot ng Pusa sa Tagiliran* (2013, poems in Filipino), *Sound Before Water* (2013, poems in English), and *A Thousand Eyes* (poems in English, 2015). Forthcoming in 2016 is his first short story collection in Filipino, *Sanga sa Basang Lupa*. He blogs at www.matangmanok.wordpress.com

**Koleka Putuma** is a theatre director, writer, and performance poet.

Her plays include *UHM* (2014), *Mbuzeni* (2015/2016), plays for young audiences which include *Ekhaya* for 2–7-year-olds and *SCOOP*, the first South African play for 2-week–12-month-old babies.

She was nominated for the Rosalie van der Gucht Prize for Best New Directors at the annual Fleur Du Cap Theatre Awards (2015). She has been named one of the young pioneers who took South Africa by storm in 2015 by the *Sunday Times*. She has recently been awarded the Pen Student Writing Prize for her poem, 'Water'.

**Sibongile Ralana** is a black writer. She is a young woman. She concerns herself with the current affairs and state of South Africa, her home. She is currently studying towards an LLB degree at the University of Cape Town. Words have always mattered to her. Words tell important and not so important stories; but they tell something. Be it the truth or lies. The writer is not so much inspired by established and renowned writers but by everyday people and how they express themselves using language.

**Arja Salafranca** has published three collections of poetry, *A Life Stripped of Illusions*, which received the Sanlam Award for poetry, *The Fire in Which We Burn*; and most recently, *Beyond Touch* (2015). Her fiction has been published online, in anthologies and journals, and is collected in her debut collection, *The Thin Line*, long-listed for the Wole Soyinka Award. She has participated in a number of writers' conferences, edited two anthologies and received awards for her poetry and fiction. She is the lifestyle editor at *The Sunday Independent* and lives in Johannesburg. Find her online at www.arjasalafranca.blogspot.com.

**Ferdie Schaller** is a retired school principal presently lecturing at the Vaal University of Technology.

**Karin Schimke** is a journalist and a poet. She writes, translates and edits for a living.

**Kori Sefeane** is 22 years old and currently studying Economics at the University of Pretoria. He writes and performs poetry part time. He started writing poetry in 2010 but only started rigorously performing in 2015. He has a passion for storytelling and word play in literature.

**Sinazo Somhlahlo**, pen/stage name Nazfloe, is a writer and spoken word performer from Butterworth, currently residing in Johannesburg. She started writing songs as a child in primary school so the transition to poetry was a natural one, writing in both English and isiXhosa. Nazfloe has graced stages such as the Muvhango 15-year celebration gala event. Inspired by the human condition, she writes about love, hate crimes, rape and the likes. She aspires to give a voice to the voiceless.

**Caitlin Spring** is currently a Creative Writing Honours student at the University of Witwatersrand. After completing her studies at the University of Cape Town she moved to Johannesburg to pursue her writing.

**David Steyn** is a writer and poet from Pretoria, South Africa. He is currently doing work in film and television. He graduated from the University of South Africa in 2015 with a Bachelor's degree in Creative Writing and Literature. Steyn lived in Los Angeles, California while he studied screenwriting and attended The Second City Training Center. He has travelled extensively through countries such as Israel, Botswana, Zambia, Namibia and Zimbabwe.

He has written several articles and reviews for South African publications such as *ATKV Taalgenoot*, *Mahala*, *Perdeby* student newspaper and *SAMusic*. Some of them appeared under his pseudonym of Karel Kopbeen. Steyn was longlisted for the Sol Plaatje European Union Poetry Award in 2015. His short stories and poetry have been featured in *New Contrast*, *The Kalahari Review*, Botsotiso 17th edition, *Ons Klyntji* magazine, *Expound* literary magazine, *Prufrock* literary magazine and on LitNet.

David was also a founding member, organiser, and co-owner of Die Dowe Digters, a monthly poetry and music session event hosted in Pretoria. For this, he appeared as a panel guest on KykNet: Flits, and on The Grind Radio as guest and later co-host. He worked as assistant production manager and performer at the 2012 and 2013 Oppikoppi festival in Northam. He has also done some background acting for South African films and TV shows such as *Musiek vir die Agtergrond*, *Ballade vir 'n Enkeling*, and *Thomas@*.

**Caitlin Stobie** is co-editor of *Epizootics*, an online literary magazine for the contemporary animal. Her poems and short stories have appeared in journals such as *Flash*, *uHlanga*, *The Kalahari Review*, Aerodrome, *New Coin*, and *Type/Cast*. She is a previous winner of the Douglas Livingstone Short Story Competition (2010) and the Heather Drummond Memorial Prize for Poetry (2012), and was recently longlisted for the Bath Flash Fiction Award (2016).

**Louella Sullivan** has learned to type poems one-handed while bouncing small babies on her lap. She did a Master's degree in Creative Writing at Rhodes University in 2014 where she completed her thesis 'Bitten' under Robert Berold. She is a History and English teacher and a part-time lecturer at Rhodes University. She has been published in Aerodrome, *New Contrast*, *New Coin* and *Itch*. Her poems have been described as "polished, poised and vivid".

**Elizabeth Trew** was born in Cape Town, went into exile and returned decades later in 1991. She taught in adult education colleges in London and Johannesburg, and has poems published in various South African poetry journals and anthologies in South Africa and England and performed at the Jozi Spoken Word Fest. A selection of her poetry is in *ISISx* (Botsotso) and in *Prodigal Daughters: Stories of*

*South African Women in Exile*, edited by Lauretta Ngcobo. She is on the editorial board of the women's writing project, *People Opposing Women Abuse* (POWA) and volunteers at a girls' shelter in Cape Town.

**Lesego Tsoho** is an enthusiastic female, who was born and bred in the small town of Vosloorus. She was raised by a single parent – her mother. She attended school at Fortune Kunene Primary School and later went to Illinge Secondary School, which is where she discovered her talent in writing.

Her zeal for writing continued to grow as she grew up. She believes that everyone has been given a talent by God. Nevertheless she believes that other people sit on their talent by will.

Lastly, she always puts a smile on your face, for one smile hides a million tears.

**Troydon Wainwright** is a deep thinker who learnt to write as a means of overcoming his dyslexia. He has won a few writing awards, including Science Fiction South Africa's Nova Short Story Contest 2009. His poetry has been published in *New Contrast* and in an anthology called *Africa's Best New Poets 2015* (Langaa RPCIG), among others. He enjoys public speaking and has been a feature poet at a number of poetry events. He is currently seeking a publisher for two of his novels and is soon to self-publish his first poetry anthology. One of his Facebook posts has gone viral.

**Athol Williams** is a poet and social philosopher from Cape Town. He was awarded the 2015 Sol Plaatje European Union Poetry Award. Athol has published three poetry collections, the most recent being *Bumper Cars*. He holds five degrees and is currently studying Political Philosophy at Oxford University.

**Sue Woodward** is a writer and editor of educational material and children's fiction. She is passionate about poetry as a creative discipline and has been writing and reading poetry for many years. She has been published in South African literary magazines, including *the Sol Plaatje European Union Poetry Anthology*. Sue lives in Muizenberg, a short walk from the sea, the mountains and the vlei. The Zandvlei estuary is the inspiration for many of her poems.

# What is the European Union (EU)?

The EU is a unique economic and political partnership between 28 European countries* that has delivered half a century of peace, stability and prosperity; helped raise living standards; launched a single European currency; and is progressively building a single Europe-wide market in which people, goods, services and capital move among Member States as freely as within a country.

Created in the aftermath of the Second World War, the first steps taken towards a union were to foster economic cooperation. Since then, the union has developed into a huge single market with the euro as its common currency. What began as a purely economic union has evolved into an organisation spanning all areas, from development aid to environmental policy.

The EU actively promotes human rights and democracy and has the most ambitious emission reduction targets for fighting climate change in the world. Thanks to the abolition of border controls between EU countries, it is now possible for people to travel freely within most of the EU.

**How does it work?**
EU Member States have set up institutions to run the EU and adopt its legislation. The main ones are:
- The European Parliament (representing the people of Europe)

---

\* Belgium, Bulgaria, Croatia, Czech Republic, Denmark, Germany, Estonia, Ireland, Greece, Spain, France, Italy, Cyprus, Latvia, Lithuania, Luxembourg, Hungary, Malta, the Netherlands, Austria, Poland, Portugal, Romania, Slovenia, Slovakia, Finland, Sweden, and the United Kingdom.

- The Council of the European Union (representing national governments)
- The European Commission (representing the common EU interest)

### Size & population
The EU is less than half the size of the United States covering some 4 million km. In terms of size, France is the EU's largest country and Malta its smallest. The EU has a population of close to 503 million people – the world's third largest after China and India.

### The EU's economy
Operating as a single market, the EU is a major world trading power. EU economic policy seeks to sustain growth by investing in transport, energy and research while minimising the impact of further economic development on the environment. Measured in terms of the goods and services it produces, its economy is bigger than that of the US.

### EU symbols
- The European flag – The 12 stars in a circle symbolise the ideals of unity, solidarity and harmony among the peoples of Europe.
- The European anthem – The melody used to symbolise the EU comes from Ludwig Van Beethoven's 9th Symphony composed in 1823.
- Europe Day – The ideas behind the EU were first put forward on 9 May 1950 by French Foreign Minister Robert Schuman. This is why 9 May is celebrated as a key date for the EU.
- The EU motto – "United in diversity".

## The EU & South Africa – a partnership of equals

Since 1994 the growing relationship between South Africa and the EU has been underpinned by the Trade, Development and Cooperation Agreement (TDCA). Closer ties between the two parties were consolidated in 2007 with the establishment of the EU-SA Strategic Partnership.

This partnership, the only one of its kind with an African country, is centred on enhanced political dialogue around issues of shared interest including climate change, the global economy, governance, bilateral trade, and peace and security matters. In line with this, its action plan encompasses sectoral cooperation on a range of issues such as climate change, environment, education, science and technology, space, trade and migration.

Summits, as well as ministerial and senior officials' meetings steer the partnership, along with the EU–South Africa Joint Cooperation Council. They provide the occasions to discuss current bilateral, regional and global issues.

The EU is South Africa's most important trading partner. In 2015, according to Eurostat, the EU was the destination of about 21% (€19.1bn) of total SA exports and the source of almost 30% (€25.5bn), of total SA imports. Manufactured goods comprise a meaningful component of SA's exports, with well over half the exports to the EU leaving SA shores in processed or semi-processed form. EU countries are also the source of some 76% of foreign direct investment (FDI) stock in South Africa.